N. 2.000.

To my Old

Building friend

Colin Jenkins.

John Coni

The Clifton Club
in Context

The Clifton Club in Context

John E Collins & Elizabeth Rosengren

The Clifton Club Company Ltd

First published in Great Britain in 1999 by
The Clifton Club Company Ltd,
22 The Mall, Clifton, Bristol BS8 4DS

Typeset in 11pt Bristol Book
Design and book production by L J S Evans
Image-setting by Micro Laser Designs, Bath

Printed in Great Britain by
Bookcraft, Midsomer Norton

British Library Cataloguing in Publication Data
A catalogue record of this book is available from the British Library

ISBN: 0 9537077 0 9

This book is dedicated to the staff at the Club over the years,
in particular Jess Barton
who, in his paternal way, looked after members
for an impressive total of sixty-two years

Contents

	Foreword	
	List of Illustrations	
	Introduction	
1	Gentlemen's Clubs	1
2	General Background to the Clifton Club	7
3	The First Clifton Club	15
4	The Second Venue	23
5	The Clifton Assembly Rooms and Hotel	32
6	Purchase of the Assembly Rooms and Royal Hotel	36
7	Alterations and Refurbishment	45
8	Nineteenth Century Building Services	51
9	Public Rooms, Family Rooms, Gentlemen's Club	59
10	The Reading Rooms	67
11	Tenants on the Mall	73
12	The Tavern in Waterloo Street	79
13	Administrative Problems	86
14	Handover to the Clifton Club Company	94
15	Nineteenth Century Communications	105
16	Getting About	111
17	Food and Drink - Nineteenth Century	123
18	Food and Drink - Twentieth Century	131
19	Having a Ball	136
20	The First World War	144
21	Squash	149
22	The Second World War	156
23	Club Members	162
24	Gentlemen's Gentlemen	171
25	Conclusion	180
	Chairmen of the Clifton Club	184

Foreword

As a new millennium approaches this is a fitting time to take stock of the efforts and decisions made by our predecessors which have given us the Clifton Club as it is today. This indeed has been the motivation of the authors and I commend this book to you in the expectation that it will help to do just that.

This account, however, is not intended to be a dry, sequential record. Instead, the authors have set the story in the context — hence the title — of the developing social and economic climate during the Club's existence over the last two centuries.

Clearly, the book is a labour of love and we are deeply indebted to John Collins, our respected fellow-member, and Elizabeth Rosengren for their research and creativity.

However, as we have learnt along the way, there is more to a book than producing the text, vital though that is. For the 'downstream' part of the project we must thank Jack Evans, ably supported by Tony Cropper, for layout and design, colour illustrations and generally for assembling the final package and putting it in the hands of the printers.

We are also grateful to the Bristol Museum and Art Gallery, the Blaise Castle Museum, Bristol, and the Mitchell Library, State Library of New South Wales, Sydney, for their permission to reproduce illustrations. In addition, thanks are due to Paul Forrest whose painting of the Club premises adorns the book jacket.

Nor should we overlook the contribution of the many talented *Punch* artists of the past, whose sharp-eyed observations of the contemporary scene help to enliven and capture key aspects of life described in the text. How times change!

Our grateful thanks are also due to the many generations of committees, members and staff who have devoted so much care and attention to the welfare of the Club, particularly those who in the last thirty years have greatly improved the interior of the premises.

The Club goes forward with confidence into the twenty-first century, knowing that the members will continue to enjoy stimulating and convivial company in elegant surroundings.

T R Pearce
Chairman

List of Illustrations

Colour

Entering the Clifton Club

Hallway and staircase i

Hallway and entrance ii

Porter's lodge

Rooflight over the main staircase

St Andrew's Church

Entrance to the churchyard iii

All that remains of the church

Francis Greenway

Portrait on a banknote iv

Plaque outside the Club premises

Prisoners in Newgate Prison, Bristol v

St James' Church, Sydney

Inside the Club

The Billiard Room vi

The Bridge Room vii

The Centenary Room viii

'The Clifton Assembly Rooms' ix

The 'Captain's Chair'

A comfortable corner

The Reading Room x, xi

The Front Bar Room

Chandeliers and mirrors xii

View of the Mall Gardens xiii

Set for lunch xiv

The Front Bar Room (contd)
The bar, ready for business *xv*
Commemorative serving dish

Artefacts
Weighing machine *xvi*
Members' postbox
Victorian armchair

Black and White

Ashmead's 1828 map of Clifton 8
St Vincent's Rocks and the Hotwells 11
St Andrew's, Clifton Parish Church 13
Birdcage Walk 17
Francis Greenway's design for the Clifton Assembly Rooms and Hotel 33
Sale notice for the 'Royal Victoria Hotel' 37
Corner building on Caledonia Place 77
Wine merchant's advertisement 82
Club premises in the 1950s 98
Victoria Rooms in Edwardian times 137

In addition, numerous *Punch* cartoons of the period are interspersed throughout the text.

Introduction

The Clifton Club — short and to the point — has been our name since the founding of the Clifton Club Rooms in 1818. The original proprietor-members would stroll through Birdcage Walk towards their new club premises, which were located close to the parish church of St Andrew's. They were proud of the exclusive nature of their enterprise. Eventually, due to the passage of time and a systematic reluctance to accept recruits, very few members remained. When the Clifton Club Rooms had literally dwindled away and closed, survivors resurrected the institution at its current premises on the Mall. Although re-christened the Clifton Subscription Rooms Association, it continued to be popularly known as the Clifton Club. When the reins were handed over to the Clifton Club Company in 1882, the matter was finally resolved and the unofficial name which had always been used — even in the minutes of the Association — was formally adopted.

An impressive stack of minute books was discovered in the basement of the Mall premises in 1980. As no-one had any idea of their existence, this was an exciting find. Records of committee meetings and accounts which date back to 1818 are written in a flowing copperplate on brittle yellowed paper bound in worn leather covers. Although it is often difficult to decipher the handwriting, these volumes have been the source of most of the relevant information in this book. Because their precise prose conveys the prim attitudes of our nineteenth century predecessors, it has been extensively quoted. Bearing in mind that these are only minutes and not works of fiction, it has been rewarding to come across colourful characters and situations — which are of course included for the reader's diversion.

Additional research has helped to provide a background for the emerging picture. With a little ingenuity and cross-referencing, it has been possible to piece together a jigsaw puzzle relating to the history of the Club and set this against the context of contemporary events. Such a history spans the most interesting period of this millennium, covering as it does every major invention in use today. During the time that the Clifton Club has been in existence (under one name or another) the Western world has progressed from a fairly primitive era to the electronic age...

1

Gentlemen's Clubs

Although nowadays it may appear an age-old tradition, the gentlemen's club has not always existed in its present form. One of the earliest references from the mid-seventeenth century implies that a 'clubbe' was a collection of like-minded people without a specific venue. The real forerunners of gentlemen's clubs were the old London coffee shops, which provided pleasant surroundings where gentlemen of means and leisure could convene and converse regularly. They were lured to their favourite establishments by the congenial company, while the quantities of newspapers and periodicals available also exerted some influence. Although the coffee shops lacked exclusivity, as anyone might be admitted within reason, in time several of them developed directly into gentlemen's clubs. In this way, such early establishments as White's, Brooks' and Boodle's came into being.

Rather more structured were the dining clubs, which flourished in eighteenth-century London and only included gentlemen with specific interests, who were invited to assemble on certain dates for learned discussions over dinner. Because the members were bound together by a common theme, many of these clubs continued to meet well into the nineteenth century, using restaurants as their venue. The Athenæum was originally founded as a dining club in 1824. When Samuel Johnson defined 'club' in his dictionary as 'an assembly of good fellows meeting under certain conditions' it was doubtless his own dining club that he had in mind. This was very much a British institution with no real counterpart in the rest of Europe.

Subscription houses were equally a British invention centred in London. However, they were more expensive to establish since they usually involved the acquisition of an aristocratic West End residence, with domestic contents including servants. It was during the second decade of the nineteenth century, after the Napoleonic Wars, that a number of new subscription houses appeared. No longer the exclusive preserve of the aristocracy, these all had slightly different specialities — for example the Travellers', or the United Services Club. Subscribers included gentry, higher officers, statesmen, intellectuals and professional men as well as numerous titled gentlemen. Additional clubs were founded in London by successive generations, but most of those which survive today are Victorian in origin.

Subscription houses or clubs quickly became an established element in London social life. The word 'club' came to mean not only an association of like-minded people, but also the venue exclusive to them. Such an institution suited the lifestyle of English gentlemen and it became a significant feature in social history. As Henry Crabb Robinson wrote, 'these great clubs have changed the character of London society and will save many a young man from the evils of a rash marriage as well as habits of dissipation.'

Thomas Walker made an early comment on the new institution in 1835:

> One of the most important changes in society is the present system of clubs. The facilities of living have been wonderfully increased by them in many ways, whilst the expense has been greatly diminished. For a few pounds a year, advantages are to be enjoyed, which no fortune except the most ample can procure... Every member has the command of an excellent library with maps; the daily papers, the principal periodicals, and every material for writing, with attendance. The building is a sort of palace, and is kept with the same exactness and comfort as a private dwelling. Every member is a master, without any of the

trouble of a master... He has the command of regular servants, without having to pay or manage them. He can have whatever meal or refreshment he wants, at all hours... In short, it is impossible to suppose a greater degree of liberty in living.

The special premises set up for the gregarious élite were like a second home and provided familiar domestic benefits. Once they were behind the mysterious façade, members could catch up with news (or sleep) in the reading room, relax with acquaintances over lunch, entertain guests, cash cheques, write letters and even arrange for accommodation at the club overnight.

At the same time, there were other advantages which may have been lacking at home. Having been elected to join a London club, members had only to pay their subscription regularly to have access to a distinguished building, devoted servants, and a large circle of potential friends. Conversation with gentlemen of like interests could have the effect of broadening horizons. And the predominantly male atmosphere allowed less formal behaviour than would have been the case in mixed company. It is hardly surprising that the clubs inspired so much respect and affection, often shown in tangible form by legacies and donations from members.

Membership of a club was like a passport, giving unprecedented opportunities for democratic socialising regardless of the diversity of backgrounds; this was one of the main attractions. As the Reverend F G Waugh commented:

> Thither resort day after day, men of intellect, adherents of art and literature, the scientist, poet, philosopher, traveller, ambassador, author, artist, theologian, statesman, the highest members of the learned professions... Nobleman, man about town, country gentleman, meet here on a social equality elsewhere unattainable.

Clubs offered great advantages, but there were also drawbacks, particularly in the culinary department. It is true that club cuisine was sometimes a source of complaint, but on the other hand, meals were much more reasonable than comparable restaurant fare. To prevent members from defaulting to local restaurants, a few of the London clubs, such as the Reform and Crockford's, made a point of importing French chefs, while Wattier's was actually founded by the Prince Regent's chef, whose exquisite cuisine could hardly be matched elsewhere in the capital.

The provision of facilities for lady guests was another way of competing with the attraction of restaurants. There might be special nights of the week allotted for female diners, or even a ladies' dining room, and in a few rare cases, ladies were admitted as members. However, this seemed to conflict with the basic nature of gentlemen's clubs and undermined one of their principal *raisons d'être*. As the distraught admiral exclaimed, on hearing of the proposed admission of women to his club, 'For God's sake, don't let them in here — it's the only place where I can get away from my family!'

In time, the concept of the gentlemen's club spread to other cities in Great Britain, where gentlemen of means and leisure felt the need of an exclusive refuge in which to commune unobserved with their own kind. In Edinburgh, the Caledonian dates from 1826. The Bath & County Club was opened in 1858. Among the very first clubs to flourish in the provinces was the original Clifton Club, founded as early as 1818 — in fact, it preceded many of the well-known London Clubs, appearing as it did with the initial wave of subscription houses in the wake of the Napoleonic Wars.

Clifton being a limited area from which to cull members, the Club did not have a specific theme like its London counterparts. Overnight accommodation was hardly necessary, though catering facilities were. Ladies were certainly not admitted, with the exception of a brief period in the 1850s when the identity of the Club was ambivalent. As soon as Clifton gentlemen had acquired exclusive rights to the premises the concession to ladies was rapidly withdrawn.

Like most of the London establishments, the Clifton Club maintained a simple and inexpensive table which was definitely not regarded as a threat by local restaurateurs. The reading room was well stocked, providing acceptable reason for visiting the premises, and the hours could subsequently be whiled away with games of cards or billiards. As there was an excellent cellar, members were in no particular hurry to abandon this oasis and often continued their conversations until the small hours, when late leavers risked being fined. This provincial club resembled its London counterparts in many respects, and answered to the same general description:

> A place where both luxurious and shabby surroundings exist, full of marvellous possessions, having servants of a kind which hardly exists elsewhere, employing ducal architecture and primitive equipment, splendid wine and indifferent food.

As in London, members appreciated the contrast with the outside world, regarding their premises as a haven from external troubles, where dignified seclusion was guaranteed. Excellent service was also a priority though in Clifton this did not extend to ironing the newspapers or boiling small change as in some of the more refined establishments of the metropolis. While sharing the same general principles, each club had its own individual traditions and characteristics.

2

General Background to the Clifton Club

The history of the Clifton Club would not be complete without reference to the growth of Clifton against the evolving background of Bristol. A brief history of the development of the area would start on the Downs above the Avon Gorge, thought to be the first locality inhabited in the region. A stone age site served as foundation for the Roman encampment and fortification which is now marked by the Observatory, while in Leigh Woods two similar stone age sites exist.

Less is known, however, of the founding of Bristol itself. Towards the end of the first millennium, under Ethelred Unrede (978-1016 AD), coins were minted at Bric-stowe — literally 'the place of the bridge' — a flourishing little town on the River Avon. The names of its four main streets remain unaltered today: Corn Street, Wine Street, Broad Street and Bridge Street. During mediæval times, resident merchants were successfully trading in cloth, hides, fish, wine, tin and iron. By the end of the fifteenth century records show that some two hundred and fifty Bristol-based merchants were trading with South West France, Spain and Portugal. The Society of Merchant Venturers was later established by a charter in 1552.

During the following centuries, the Society played an important part in governing the city, as many of the

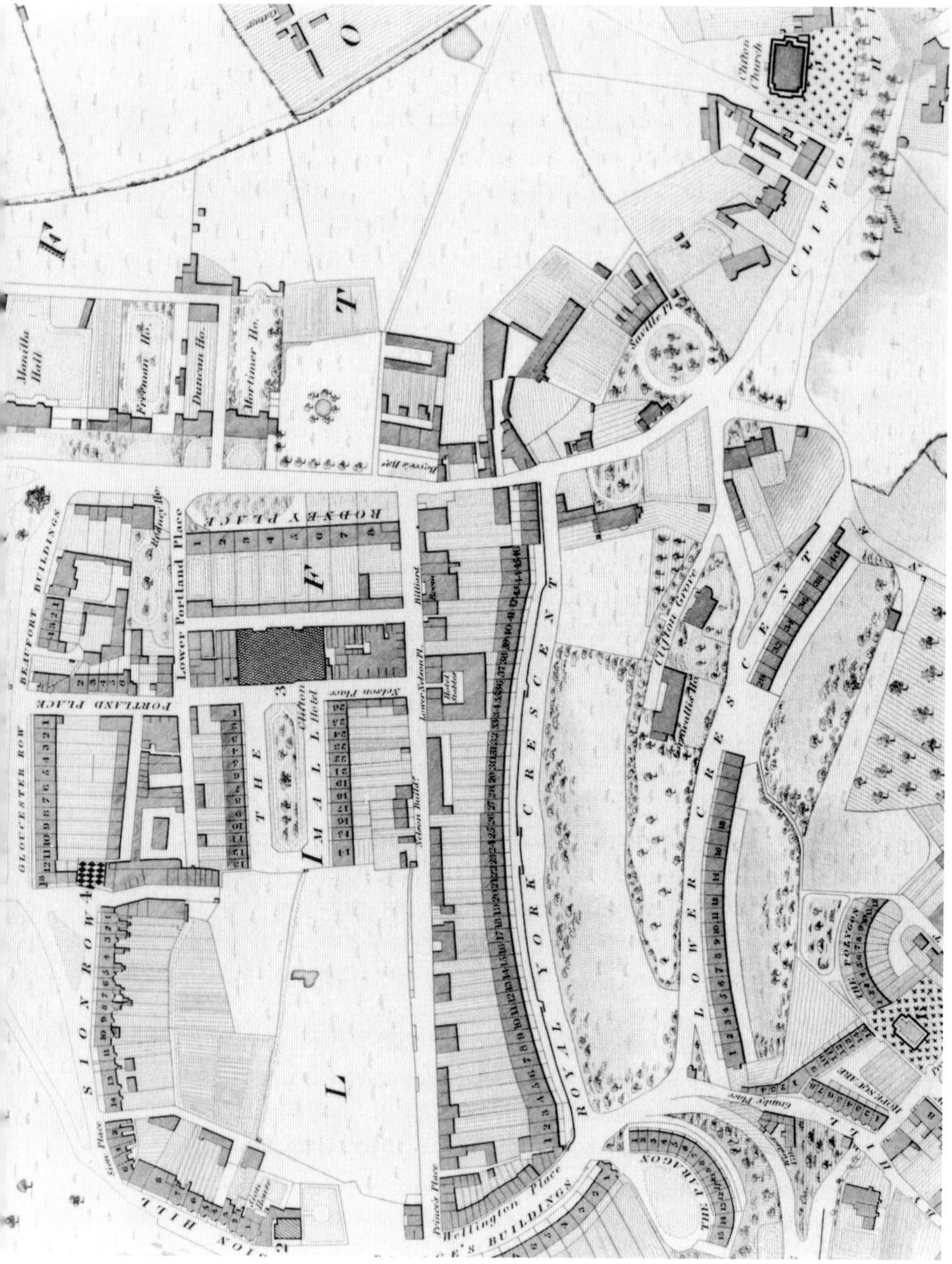

Ashmead's 1828 map of Clifton. With the map turned to normal viewing angle, the original Club site lies to the left of Clifton Church (bottom right), while the present building occupies the block above the centre of the map marked as '3, Clifton Hotel'

merchants were also members of the Corporation. Merchants tended to run their businesses from the town houses where they lived, situated close to the port of Bristol. Although the quays were the particular responsibility of the Merchant Venturers, it was the Corporation that generally administered the port. As much of the civic income consisted of taxes imposed on trading ships in the docks, it was desirable that the maximum number of ships should be accommodated.

By the start of the eighteenth century, the port of Bristol was the second largest in England. The Merchant Venturers used a percentage of their profits to extend the quays and construct new docks, but their efforts were not sufficient to keep Bristol near the top of the list. By the end of the century, due in part to the industrialisation of Lancashire, it had been superseded by half a dozen other ports, among them Liverpool. The Society considered increasing the capacity of the port of Bristol by converting all the quays into floating docks and creating a new dam at Redcliffe. Another of their problems was the fact that Parliament was passing Free Trade Acts, which meant that they could no longer keep all trading profits to themselves.

On emerging from the middle ages, England had been essentially a collection of agricultural communities with a total population of four million at the start of the sixteenth century. During that century the population rose by 38% to five and a half million. The seventeenth century brought developments in trade and industry which led to the expansion of existing towns. At that time the inhabitants of Bristol numbered between twenty-five and thirty thousand, in common with the three other major cities — York, Norwich and Southampton. Visitors compared the city of Bristol with London and Pepys commented that it was 'in every respect another London'. However, there was a considerable difference in size, as it is known that half a million people were living in the capital by the start of the eighteenth century.

A remarkable increase in population took place during that century. Figures for England rose to ten million, while the inhabitants of Bristol more than doubled, reaching sixty thousand by the year 1800. To accommodate all these residents the city expanded towards the north and west. The Society of Merchant Venturers could no longer concentrate exclusively on the administration of the port and enrichment of the mediæval city, but also turned their attention to managing properties in Clifton and Hotwells. By the late seventeenth century the Society had expended £1,705 to become owners of 75% of the Manor of Clifton. This was largely agricultural land which the merchants initially leased for periods of ninety-nine years.

The population explosion which occurred in England as a whole during the eighteenth century was more than reflected in Clifton, where the two hundred and fifty inhabitants of this rural area increased to one thousand four hundred in just seventy years. This obviously meant the creation of new roads and a start to the building programme which would transform the green fields of the Manor to the urban area we know today. As Clifton developed, the Society acted as planning authority in addition to maintaining the roads for the new residents. In time, many of the merchants decided to move from the city centre to this western hill overlooking the docks.

Apart from being a good vantage point for resident merchants, Clifton possessed another asset — the spring known as the Hotwell which gushed from below St Vincent's Rocks at a rate of sixty gallons per minute, with a temperature of 76°F. This spring was located some three metres above the river at low tide, but disappeared when the tide rose. By the mid-seventeenth century the Hotwell water had become renowned for its medicinal properties, being allegedly effective in cases of 'kidney problems, hot livers, feeble brains and red pimply faces'.

When the Merchant Venturers became principal landowners in the Clifton area, they managed to have the Hotwell included in the purchase. However, the full potential of the Hotwell spring was not realised and its development was left to leaseholders, the first of whom paid only ten shillings per annum. Eventually the spring was surrounded by a high wall to prevent it from being submerged at high tide. Its exploitation and the development of the surrounding complex were then delegated to a group of leaseholders with

St Vincent's Rocks and the Hotwells; from an etching by Nicholas Pocock circa 1785

a ninety-nine year lease at £5 per annum. As a result, Hotwell House was built on a promontory to accommodate a pump house and provide for the numerous visitors attracted to Clifton throughout the period when spas were in vogue.

During the eighteenth century, the popularity of the Hotwell increased to such an extent that it became necessary to build more residential accommodation. To cater for long-stay guests who wished to avoid the steep return climb into Clifton, the area in immediate proximity to the spring was developed, notably Hotwells and Dowry Square. However, some of the visitors preferred to commute daily from Clifton on the Hill, and residential accommodation was duly built for them alongside that of the merchants.

Towards the end of the eighteenth century, when the fashion for spas had passed its zenith, the Merchant Venturers belatedly considered further developing the Hotwell themselves. A half-hearted attempt was made to export Hotwell water bottled in Bristol Blue glass, but prices rose considerably and business flagged. Moreover, there was competition from another source of Hotwell water discovered by a resident on Sion Hill while drilling to locate a domestic water supply. A second pump was constructed over this more accessible Hotwell water. Neither of the two pump houses is extant today, the first having been demolished when the promontory on which it stood was removed as an obstruction to shipping, while the second was eventually incorporated into the St Vincent's Rocks Hotel.

By 1820 the original Hotwell was running at a loss. It even seemed that the quality of the water was deteriorating. Eventually the Hotwell was taken over by the Corporation, which must have been a relief to the Merchant Venturers. The first pump house having been demolished in 1867, only the name of the surrounding district, Hotwells, remains as a clue to the former location of the fashionable eighteenth-century spa.

During the latter years of the nineteenth century, a final attempt was made to exploit Hotwell water and a third pump house was erected near the newly constructed Suspension Bridge, adjacent to the Grand Spa Hotel (now the Avon Gorge Hotel). It was an elegant building with columns of Swiss marble, a music gallery, a lounge and hot baths, its focal point being the marble fountain from which the original water gushed. Two houses in nearby Princes Buildings provided such additional refinements as Turkish, Russian and Hydrotherapy baths, which all made use of the naturally hot water supply. If this development had taken place while thermal resorts were in vogue it would doubtless have been a success. However, as the venture was mistimed by a whole century, the third pump house was eventually closed down, allowed to fall into disrepair and virtually forgotten.

Clifton is essentially a late eighteenth-century creation, built by affluent merchants to accommodate their own families as well as visitors in search of a health cure. Many merchants opted for residences in the new terraces and crescents which offered splendid views of shipping in the port below. While the port prevented further expansion in a southerly direction, the natural boundary of the Avon Gorge limited the development of Clifton to the west. At that time the river was crossed (when the tide was in) by means of a ferry, which entailed the negotiating of cliffs on either side. The inconvenience of this crossing obviously inspired the concept of bridging the Gorge.

In 1754 a public-spirited wine merchant, William Vick, left £1,000 to the Society, on the assumption that, if wisely invested, the sum would eventually be sufficient to finance a bridge project. However, this generous gesture has since been eclipsed by the name of Brunel, who designed the resulting Suspension Bridge. Thirty-five years were to elapse between the competitions for an acceptable design and the opening of the Bridge in 1864. During this time, all kinds of difficulties were experienced, from inadequate finance to Brunel's premature death — which ironically revived public interest in the abandoned project and brought about its completion. The new link meant that more residential accommodation could be built in Leigh Woods, while it also improved road connections with the port of Bristol. Clifton was no longer a hill-top development with access from Bristol only.

St Andrew's, Clifton Parish Church, close by the site of the original Clifton Club, as it was before the Second World War

The suburb was opened up in a different way when the Clifton Rocks Railway was inaugurated in 1893. Two cars, operated by water balance, could carry passengers up and down the cliff face via a tunnel cut through the limestone. To one side of the lower exit was a small station on the Port and Pier Railway line which had been built in the middle of the nineteenth century, giving access to Portishead. To the other side lay a tram terminal which offered a service to Bristol via Hotwells. By the 1890s there were sufficient residents in Clifton to provide a constant flow of passengers for the Rocks Railway — four hundred and thirty thousand were carried in the first year alone.

This was very different to the situation prevailing during the previous century, when the Manor of Clifton had mainly housed a sparse rural population living in small dwellings scattered over the Downs, around the modest parish church of St Andrew's. Rebuilt in 1654, and further enlarged during the early eighteenth century, this church was the oldest building in Clifton. By contrast, Boyce's Buildings would have been the most recent construction at that time. There was no sign of the well-known crescents and terraces which were to rise from the stretches of green grass where sheep were still grazing. It is thanks to the planning of the Society of Merchant Venturers in the 1780s and the affluence of their members that the suburb was developed so rapidly and to such a superior architectural standard.

3

The First Clifton Club

In the provinces, the establishment of gentlemen's clubs reflected the new trends in London. Due to the relatively late development of Clifton the founding of a club was not suggested until 1818. During that year, subscriptions were invited from 'Gentlemen who have an inclination to establish the convenience of a Reading, Card and Billiard Room in Clifton'.

On 3 October 1818, Sir Richard Vaughan presided over a meeting held at the Clifton Hotel, a monumental building which had been erected only a few years previously to overlook the elegant Mall Gardens and receive visitors of distinction. (By a twist of fate, this hotel was to change its function within decades and become the present home of the Clifton Club.) At the meeting, it was decided to acquire a site in the vicinity of the Parish Church of St Andrew's (then situated near Birdcage Walk), in order to erect premises for a gentlemen's social club.

It had been ascertained that £1,000 would be sufficient to fund the enterprise, and it was therefore proposed that a total of twenty subscribers should each contribute £50. On calling over the names of the intended Subscribing Proprietors, it was found that there were fifty-one in all.

The site was purchased forthwith and building of the new premises commenced. Meanwhile, on 12 December

1818, another meeting was held at the Clifton Hotel to agree Rules and Regulations for the government of the Club and management of the property. Sir Richard Vaughan, together with eighteen other gentlemen, drew up the following:

1. The Subscribing Proprietors of the Clifton Club shall not exceed eighty members.

2. There shall be twelve Trustees in whom the property of the Club shall be vested who shall have power to adopt such measures by investing money or otherwise as may appear to them necessary for the interest of the Club. And when the Trustees are reduced by death to four, the Trust shall be filled up by a General Meeting of the Proprietors to the original number of twelve, and so on for ever.

3. The original Committee chosen at a General Meeting of the subscribers held the 24th October 1818 shall be permanent until one year after the completion of the Club Rooms, at the expiration of which time, two of its members shall retire and the vacancies be filled up by ballot at a General Meeting of the Proprietors, not less than fifteen being present, and two fresh members shall annually be elected in like manner.

4. The Committee shall have the power of calling a General Meeting of the Proprietors whenever they shall deem it requisite. All notices of such meetings shall be signed by three of its members and be posted in the Public Reading Room at least ten days previous to the day of meeting.

5. The Committee shall have the power of admitting or rejecting any newly proposed Proprietor and of fixing the prices of shares according to their discretion.

6. A General Meeting of the Proprietors shall be called as soon as the building is complete and the Rooms furnished, when an account of the cost shall be laid before them.

7. A General Meeting of the Proprietors shall be held annually on the first Monday of the month which shall be twelve months after the above meeting is held, when the year's accounts of receipts and disbursements shall be laid before them and the surplus if any after paying all the charges shall be appropriated as the majority of the members present shall appoint.

Birdcage Walk; the original Clifton Club building is among the trees on the left. Clifton Parish Church is off the picture to the right

8. On the decease of any Subscribing Proprietor the Committee shall dispose of his share to an eligible purchaser. If no such purchaser can be found within six months after the decease of such Proprietor the value of such share to be fixed by the Committee not exceeding the amount of his subscriptions shall be paid to his representatives.

9. Each Proprietor shall pay an annual subscription of three guineas commencing from 1st of June 1819.

10. Any person residing at or in the vicinity of Clifton wishing to become an annual Subscriber to the Rooms may be admitted by the Committee on paying an annual subscription of five guineas.

11. Gentlemen visiting Clifton wishing to become members for a short time shall be proposed by three Proprietors and ballotted for by not less than eleven. The name of the candidate signed by three Proprietors to be posted in the Reading Room one week previous to the ballot. On admission of such members, the three

Proprietors shall be answerable for their subscription. One black ball in eleven to exclude.

12. Individuals admitted under the foregoing rule shall be subscribers for three, six, nine or twelve months, paying a subscription of two guineas for three months, four guineas for six months, five guineas for nine months and six guineas for twelve months.

13. All subscriptions to be paid to the Treasurer whose receipt shall be deemed sufficient.

14. The Club Rooms shall be annually let by the Committee to a respectable person to the advantage and comfort of the Proprietors and Subscribers.

15. The Club Rooms shall be open every week day from 10 in the morning until 12 o'clock at night. The Reading Room only shall be open on Sundays from 1 till 5 o'clock pm.

16. There shall be three London daily and one Sunday newspaper, one Irish and two provincial papers, Navy and Army lists, magazines etc etc.

17. No paper or book shall be taken out of the Reading Room under forfeiture of one guinea.

18. No cards shall be played in the News or Reading Rooms or in the Billiard Room.

19. The games at Billiards to be paid for by the players, cards and candles by the persons calling for them, to the Keeper of the Rooms, at rates to be fixed upon by the Committee.

20. No member is on any account to bring a dog into the Rooms.

21. Any Proprietors, annual or casual member infringing the foregoing rules to suffer expulsion if upon investigation of the case the Committee shall so order and determine and all monies advanced by him, either as purchase or subscription, shall be forfeited for the benefit of the Club.

22. Each Proprietor shall sign his name to these Rules in testimony of his fully agreeing to abide by them, in a book

provided for the purpose and kept by the Committee.

23. All Rules may be altered and amended or additional rules made at any General Meeting at which a majority of the Proprietors are present, one month's notice of the proposed alteration or addition being given at a previous General Meeting and in the notice posted in the Reading Room.

On 31 August 1819, only ten months after the original proposal to found a club, another meeting was called at the Clifton Hotel to declare the new premises finished and ready to receive the billiard tables. In the worn leather-bound book which contains copperplate minutes of the meeting, it is recorded that 'the sum of £1,839.10.4d had been paid and that after paying the contractor the balance of his account, there would only remain in hands of the Treasurer about £100'. As the complete furnishing of the Rooms was estimated at between £450 and £500 (including two billiard tables at £230), the Committee announced their decision to increase the cost per share to £58. The additional sum would eventually be repaid to each Subscribing Proprietor by the appropriation of subscriptions from future members.

By 25 October 1819 the new Club Rooms were clearly in use, as a Committee Meeting was held on those premises. According to the minutes of this meeting, further attempts were made to create an orderly framework for club activities: prices were set for piquet and whist cards and rules laid down for temporary subscribers. To economise on the price of candles, no games were to commence after midnight and closing time was fixed at 12.30 am. By gradual amendment of the rules all potential loopholes were being dealt with.

At a General Meeting held on 3 April 1824 it was announced that new arrangements would have to be made with regard to the resident Manager of the Club Rooms, Mr Eames, who was paying an annual rent of £130. Accordingly it was

resolved that in consequence of the falling off of the receipts of the Club Rooms having rendered Mr Eames unable to continue as rentee of the Rooms upon the present terms, he be henceforth allowed £87 per annum out of which he is to pay the Boy and the

> Charwoman. The Treasurer to pay Taxes and all other expenses and to take to all the income of the Club Rooms.

Six years later, the Club Manager was so dissatisfied that he gave notice. One of his grievances was the very late hours kept by members who persisted in ignoring the ban on games commenced after midnight.

Instead of reinforcing law and order to promote the smooth running of the Club, the Committee appears to have reduced subscription rates, thereby giving rise to financial problems as well. Less income was generated for the Club, and some of this was made available for the buying back of proprietors' shares at £20 each. The original members formed an exclusive and decreasing group which did not welcome outsiders. Within two decades, the Club had become financially unviable. A special meeting was convened on 15 April 1850, for the purpose of

> receiving a statement of the accounts, of electing a Committee and of determining on the expedience of making new arrangements for the management of the property. It will be proposed to the meeting to authorise the premises being let or sold as may appear desirable.

Only twenty members attended this important meeting, at which the Treasurer presented a summary of the Club's history with reasons for the contemporary financial problems, finally proposing realistic solutions:

> The Clifton Club was formed in the year 1818. By the resolutions of a meeting held in December 1819 it appears that the cost of the land, building, furniture and other disbursements was then ascertained at £3,159.4.6d, which was raised by the creation of sixty-three shares of £50 each with annual subscriptions etc to that time.
>
> That by the original Rules each Proprietor paid an annual subscription of three guineas and non-Proprietors five guineas.
>
> That in the earlier years a dividend on the shares was declared and paid to the Proprietors.

That in the year 1826 all dividends ceased, and also all subscriptions by Proprietors, who have consequently been admitted free in right of their shares, and that the terms of admission for subscribers have been from time to time reduced to the present scale.

That up to the year 1844 the receipts of the establishment sustained its expenses and afforded a surplus from which the shares of Proprietors dying or leaving Clifton were purchased, and from which also a fund amounting to £700 and upward had accumulated which was then invested in Exchequer Bills, with a balance in the hands of the Treasurer.

That with this fund the premises were altered and improved in the year 1844 at a considerable expense.

That from January 1844 to the present period [April 1850] the annual expenses have far exceeded the receipts in each year, the total deficiency upon the last five years having been ascertained at the sum of £392.8.2d and the average loss on the last three years at £110 per annum.
The financial position of the concern at present is as follows. £100 is invested in an Exchequer Bill and there is a cash balance in the hands of the Treasurer of nearly £100, a considerable part of which will be required to defray the expenses of the current year.

The Proprietors are reduced by the purchase of shares to thirty-six. Of this number two-thirds are either non-resident, deceased or do not avail themselves of the advantage of the Rooms.

Under the foregoing circumstances it is suggested whether it has not become necessary to dissolve the Club and if so whether the premises should not be sold and an arrangement made with the present subscribers for closing the Rooms from 24th June next. Under any circumstances a Committee must be appointed to conduct the affairs, either for continuance or winding up.

It was unanimously decided to dispose of the premises by public auction, tender or private contract or, failing this, to let the Rooms either furnished or unfurnished. The Committee was given *carte blanche*. Eight months later, the Treasurer was able to report that the sale had been concluded:

> That the purchase money amounting to the sum of £1,000 had been received.
>
> That the billiard tables, furniture etc had realised on sale by auction £103.16.6d and that the balance in favour of the Proprietors on the general account, as distinguished from that appertaining to the sale, amounts to £190.18.6d, which three several sums, after deducting the expenses of the sale and its completion, and those of winding up the affairs of the Club upon its dissolution, give a balance of £1,208.3.0d, which balance will afford to each shareholder £34.7.0d as his proportion.
>
> On a careful examination of the books and documents of the Society it appears that, of the original sixty-three shares, twenty-eight have been purchased by the Society, which leave thirty-five as existing, the holders of which are entitled to participate in the division.

It would appear that the premises, which were adjacent to Clifton Parish Church, were purchased by the Reverend Mr Marshall and his Churchwardens, possibly for use as an annexe. It has been impossible to locate the Title Deeds of the property, although these were mentioned in the minutes of a Clifton Club meeting held on 11 May 1843 as 'deposited in a tin box and placed at the Old Bank under the care of Messrs Baillie Ames Baillie'.

In any case, nothing else remains of the original Rooms today. Together with Clifton Parish Church, they were destroyed during the Second World War. Only the headstones of the churchyard survive to indicate the spot near Birdcage Walk where the first parish church once stood.

4

The Second Venue

The demise of such an institution as the Clifton Club Rooms after thirty-two years appeared so final that hardly any trace of it might be expected to remain in local history. However, this demise proved to be only temporary. Memories of the disbanded club encouraged a few Clifton gentlemen to take advantage of an opportunity which arose in 1850. The former Hotel and Assembly Rooms in the Mall, Clifton, had deteriorated to a point where the building was offered for sale. As the accommodation was suitable, this property was eventually purchased, and the Clifton Club was reconstituted in the premises which it occupies today.

The history of the impressive building in the Mall is of general interest, while that of its architect and builder, Francis Greenway, is worth recounting in some detail. The original concept dates to the start of the nineteenth century when Clifton was still an expanding spa. On 16 May 1806 a meeting of the local nobility and gentry was called to consider a proposal for building a new Assembly Room, which would provide an attractive venue for the increasing numbers of both residents and visitors to the resort. At that time West Mall (then known as the Mall) and Caledonia Place were only half their present length, with green fields in the immediate vicinity. Between these two isolated Georgian terraces and Rodney Place it was decided to build the Assembly Room in conjunction with a Hotel.

Just six weeks later, unhampered by the delays of modern planning permission, it was recorded that:

> The Foundation for a new Assembly Room is already begun at the East end of the Mall at Clifton; the design by Mr Greenway, architect, of this city, does great credit to his abilities, and will be a handsome public building, and will do honour to the liberality and taste of those who have patronised and subscribed to it.

The name of Francis Greenway was later to become a household word in Australia, where he is known today as the Father of Australian Architecture. Over there his portrait has even featured on a ten dollar bill, while ironically in his homeland he has virtually been forgotten. Greenway's only surviving building in Britain is in fact the current premises of the Clifton Club, originally the Assembly Rooms and Hotel on the Mall, Clifton.

The Greenways had specialised in stone masonry for generations, a branch of the family having settled in the Bristol and Bath area where excellent stone was quarried. One member of the clan, Thomas Greenway, designed and built Beau Nash's Palace and, with his sons, participated in the building of eighteenth-century Bath.

Another who diverged from the traditional family craft was Francis Howard Greenway, whose special gifts made him far more than a stonemason — an 'architect of eminence' in fact. A fourth son, born on 20 November 1777, he was of relatively short and stocky build with a slight stoop. His self-portrait in crayons shows a rather obstinate face with aquiline nose, hazel-brown eyes and light-coloured wavy hair. In relating to people, Francis Greenway could be petulant, tactless and arrogant. He had a talent for alienating friends and rousing the hostility of strangers. It was these combined traits that undermined his professional success, causing much suffering both to him and his family.

In 1805, at the age of twenty-seven, Francis set up a partnership with his oldest brother, and advertised for business in Felix Farley's *Bristol Journal*:

> MESSRS GREENWAY beg leave to inform their friends and the public that they have opened a room and a yard at No 7 Limekiln Street... All orders for marble monuments, chimney pieces and every kind of ornamental stonework shall be carefully attended to and executed in the most artist-like manner. Designs for houses, lodge gates and every part of domestic architecture may be seen at the office drawn by F Greenway — who takes this opportunity of offering his services to the public in the capacity of architect, statuary and landscape gardener.

Together with a third brother, they made ornaments for the aristocracy, repaired Mangotsfield Church and were generally kept very busy. Francis must have felt that he was on the way to fame when he accepted the important commission of designing and building a civic centre for Clifton: the Assembly Rooms and Grand Hotel.

The building had been erected and roofed by April 1809, when financial disaster struck, according to a notice which appeared in the *Bristol Gazette*, convening creditors of Francis Greenway, 'architect and builder'. The following week, a notice in the *Bristol Mirror* announced a sale by auction at Mr Greenway's premises in Ashton to dispose of his household furniture and a valuable collection of books. The three brothers had already been declared bankrupt. To satisfy some of the creditors, building materials remaining in several unfinished houses in the Lower (Cornwallis) Crescent were valued and sold. In addition, officials removed from Limekiln Street 'all the valuable stock of marble in blocks, handsome chimney pieces, slabs and valuable ornaments, together with building materials including stone and a collection of figures in plaster of Paris, some in imitation of bronze, from the models of the ancients, and very scarce and valuable'.

The vogue for 'taking the waters' of the Hotwell had started a wave of development on the green hill of Clifton, with several of the Georgian terraces being commenced simultaneously. However, the Napoleonic Wars had put an end to this activity, which was only resumed in the early nineteenth century at the time when the Greenways were setting up their partnership. It is quite possible that their insolvency was connected with work on the unfinished houses in Cornwallis Crescent, from which their building materials were taken and sold.

The two older brothers quietly survived the experience of bankruptcy, subsequently building the churches of Frenchay and Downend. However, Francis was adversely affected. Although he could have cut his losses in the same way and made a fresh start as an architect, he seemed determined to vindicate himself and pay off creditors (even though this might be by devious means and was quite unnecessary). A certain Colonel Doolan had paid thirteen hundred guineas for a building in Cornwallis Crescent finished by Francis Greenway, the contract for which had been mislaid. Creditors were satisfied with arbitration on the dispute which resulted, but Greenway was not. He maintained that an additional £250 had been promised, and that a solicitor (who strongly denied the allegation) had recorded this on the contract.

Although the evidence was rejected by the arbitrators, Greenway arrogantly persisted. He published a notice to the effect that anyone returning the lost contract would receive a reward of ten guineas. Strangely enough, in January 1812 the original contract was anonymously left in the vestibule of the Bristol Mercury office, with the following note upon it, ostensibly in the solicitor's handwriting: 'Colonel Doolan to pay Mr Greenway two hundred and fifty pounds for the house as it is, in addition to the thirteen hundred guineas for finishing the house, as follows'.

When Greenway insisted that the Colonel should be prosecuted, it was proved that the memorandum was a forgery — although contemporaries failed to understand the architect's motive. In fact, he could not bear to lose a battle with opponents whom he despised, and it would seem that he was prepared to go to the lengths of forgery to be proved right and restore his public reputation.

However, his action had the opposite effect, completely changing the course of his life. Greenway was promptly committed to Newgate Prison. His crime was elaborated in 'a bill of indictment which consisted of such a number of skins of parchment sewn together that it was one continuous roll, extending in length fifty-five feet'. In March 1812 Greenway found himself in the dock at the Bristol Assizes, pleading guilty to the crime of forgery. He was sentenced to death by hanging. However, doubtless due to the influence of friends, this sentence was later commuted to one of transportation to Botany Bay for fourteen years.

After his trial, Greenway spent a further seventeen months in prison before setting sail for New South Wales on the *General Hewitt* (together with 295 other convicts), as part of a convoy of three convict ships. The daily ration of water for all purposes was only three pints per man, while the food was soon crawling with vermin, like the ship itself. During the six-month voyage, conditions deteriorated even more. Prisoners and their bedding were soaked by sudden rain squalls, so that mildew and constant damp had to be endured in addition to the dysentery which broke out. On leaving Rio de Janeiro, sickness claimed an increasing number of convicts when sanitation and fumigation routines were discontinued. In all thirty-four corpses had been consigned to the waves by the time that the *General Hewitt* docked at Sydney Cove. When the sickly, gaunt and filthy survivors had been inspected, shocked officials reported back to Governor Macquarie, who used this appalling example of convict transportation in his campaign to reform the system.

The humanitarian Governor, ensured that convicts were unchained, housed in the dilapidated convict settlement, issued with clothing and given a generous weekly ration of meat and wholemeal bread. Provided they behaved well and carried out their allotted work, they were treated 'on a footing of equality with the general population'. Sentences were often shortened and the reformed prisoners could then become worthy members of society without stigma. Convicts and ex-convicts were employed in most capacities, the majority of trades and professions being well represented. However, Governor Macquarie was in desperate need of an architect to construct municipal landmarks in this incipient township, and had been awaiting the answer to an appeal sent to London:

> It would be highly necessary and very desirable that a government architect should be sent out to this country to plan

> and superintend the erection of all public buildings, and I specifically entreat your Lordship will send out a well-qualified person of this description to the colony as soon as possible.

The arrival of Francis Greenway seemed to be the answer, and the letter of introduction written for him by an admiral further ensured his welcome. However, Governor Macquarie, who had only been in office for three years, had a number of major problems to solve before he could concentrate on architecture. Five months elapsed before Greenway was asked to collaborate on the transformation of the unplanned settlement that was Sydney. Every type of public building was needed. The site, which included a harbour, headlands, a sheltered valley and the backdrop of the Blue Mountains, was ideal. And a variety of building materials, from stone to oak, was available locally.

Governor Macquarie first requested that Greenway should copy a drawing for the proposed town hall and court house. Somewhat offended and belligerent as ever, the talented convict replied:

> I will immediately copy the drawing Your Excellency requested me to do, notwithstanding it is rather painful to my mind as a professional man to copy a building that has no claim to classical proportion or character.

After some initial misunderstanding, the Governor realised Greenway's potential as an architect. His luck changed and providence seemed to offer him a second chance. Though still a convict, he was appointed in 1816 as Acting Government Architect and Assistant Engineer, at a salary of three shillings a day. He was provided with a house for his wife and family, (who had eventually arrived in the settlement on board another ship), rations, coal, a horse and a convict-servant. Soon after this appointment, the architect who had been officially selected for the colony arrived, Mr Henry Kitchen aged twenty-three. He proved to be no great threat to the already established Greenway, who did not feel that his professional standing was in any way diminished by deportation.

Trained in the late-Georgian style, he had produced one

conventional building in England, the current premises of the Clifton Club. On being transferred to Sydney, he did not simply continue in the same vein, but took into account local architectural conditions before adapting his style. The effect of climate upon indifferent building materials, together with the inferior quality of available workmanship, had to be considered. As a result, Greenway began to design buildings with a more individual stamp. Australia brought out his ingenuity and genius, and he clearly improved the building techniques of the colony.

Although Greenway tended to think big, nothing was too small to attempt. He designed the obelisk and a fountain in Macquarie Place, the Macquarie Lighthouse, the water supply and sewers, the quays and even a cross-harbour bridge. His surviving work includes three churches (St James', Sydney, St Matthew's, Windsor and St Luke's, Liverpool), the Hyde Park Barracks (now a museum), the Hospital, the Georgian School and many other buildings now demolished. His least original structures were in the fashionable Gothic style — the Government Stables (now the Conservatorium of Music), Fort Macquarie (replaced by the Opera House), Dawe's Battery and the tollgate on Brickfield Hill.

Greenway produced his best work in a period of only six years, while employed as Government Architect under Macquarie's sponsorship. During this time there were endless problems with sabotage of buildings by workmen and quarrels with engineers, contractors and government officials. Simultaneously, Macquarie was reprimanded by the Minister in London for erecting buildings that were too grandiose and costly for a settlement colonised by convicts, and a Commissioner was sent out to investigate.

There was always trouble in Greenway's vicinity, doubtless provoked by his aggressive nature and his habit of adapting the truth to suit his own purposes. His numerous indignant letters to the press and frequent lawsuits suggest that he alienated many people. On one occasion, a certain captain found him so infuriating that he administered a dramatic horse-whipping.

Having been relieved of his official post, Greenway was

free to build up a private practice while retaining the use of the centrally-situated family house granted to him by the Governor. However, he still expended excess energy on personal battles. Becoming particularly resentful over the fact that he had not received a percentage on any of his buildings for the colony, he calculated that the balance due should be £11,232.15s. He persistently hoped for some tangible acknowledgment of Macquarie's gratitude, forgetting that, as a former convict, he had already been very generously treated.

After the Governor's resignation and shortly before his departure, Greenway wrote to him requesting a gift of building land. By now exasperated with such ungrateful behaviour, continual quarrels and lack of respect, Macquarie refused to grant him more than eight hundred acres outside Sydney, although half-a-dozen cows were included. Greenway, who was very disappointed, wrote to both Macquarie and his successor. Provoked beyond endurance, Macquarie disdainfully received the demanding little architect and made him a final offer: this was to reimburse his accumulated travel expenses if an affidavit were sworn. However, in spite of his persistence, Greenway did not succeed in obtaining the money. As private clients dwindled, he evidently fell on hard times again. In 1824 the newspapers announced that his furniture and household effects would be seized and auctioned. This has a familiar ring. It will be recalled that the architect had received the same ignominious treatment in Bristol, fifteen years earlier.

Another parallel with previous events in Bristol occurred after Macquarie's death, when Greenway commenced building on the land where his rent-free house stood, maintaining that this was in accordance with a private agreement between himself and the late Governor. He was apparently in possession of a document which endorsed this and bore the words 'Approved. L Macquarie'. When this document was produced in order to prove the point, complete with the added words, it seemed that history was repeating itself. The new Governor refused to sanction such a dubious claim to crown land and instead made repeated efforts to evict Greenway and his family from their home.

On his wife's death, Greenway resorted to the illegal sale of the crown land which he still occupied, and subsequently lost any claim to the house. A period of obscurity followed, punctuated only by occasional polemics in the press, before he relinquished the fight. He died at the age of sixty in relative disgrace.

In spite of squandering so much energy in aggression, Greenway managed to establish himself as the 'Father of Australian Architecture' in only six years, leaving beautifully proportioned buildings conceived on a monumental scale for a city which, in the early nineteenth century, did not exist outside his own imagination.

5

The Clifton Assembly Rooms and Hotel

Francis Greenway's monumental creation in The Mall is his only building in the United Kingdom. It was started at a propitious time, the banks having recovered from the financial crisis brought about by the Napoleonic Wars in the 1790s. Evidence of the emergency was visible all over Clifton in the form of unfinished or derelict houses which had been abandoned during that decade by the many speculating builders who were bankrupted. At the end of the eighteenth century some five hundred houses which had been commenced in the area were still awaiting completion.

Although the first proposal to build Assembly Rooms in Clifton had been made in 1792, it had failed to obtain the necessary support from local subscribers. The idea lay dormant through the troubles, to be resurrected by a wealthy Huguenot, John Lewis Auriol, in 1806, when the nobility and gentry of Clifton were invited to attend a meeting on 16 May to consider his proposal. Having gained their consent to a building on the Mall site, Auriol engaged the young Greenway, who was then advertising his services as an architect. The scale of the project must have appealed to Greenway, who rapidly designed the building and produced the grandiose elevation drawing recently discovered among mounds of old documents relating to the Assembly Rooms. This elevation was drastically revised, but elements of the scheme, particularly the central feature dominated by the

Francis Greenway's design for the Clifton Assembly Rooms and Hotel; elevation facing The Mall

pediment, were retained. Unfortunately, there is no surviving plan of the interior.

In accordance with the practice at that time, the architect was also regarded as builder and played a very substantial role in erecting a structure, even to the point of providing building materials. By completing unfinished houses in the area, Greenway managed to remain solvent between 1806 and 1809. At this point, the juggling of capital failed, and he joined the ranks of bankrupt builders himself.

Auriol parted company with the unfortunate architect, who embarked on the prolonged legal battle which was to end in his transportation. Meanwhile, the building, which had been roofed and was more or less finished externally, was offered either for sale or lease. It is uncertain whether the interior can be ascribed to Greenway, as another architect, Joseph Kay, spent two years completing the work. Because of the ignominious fate of his predecessor, Kay was subsequently referred to as the architect responsible for the whole project. Had Greenway been aware of this as he awaited trial in Newgate Prison, he would surely have been most indignant.

Building work was eventually finished, having been in progress for a total of five and a half years, and the combined Assembly Rooms and Auriol Hotel were opened with great ceremony on 21 November 1811. The building was described as 'spacious and elegant' by the *Guide to All the Watering Places,* which mentioned that the Assembly Rooms comprised 'a noble reception saloon and tea-room, with convenient lobbies, a billiard room etc', while the Hotel offered:

> Every accommodation for both families and individuals, even to sets of apartments/drawing rooms, a coffee room; a shop for pastry and confectionery, with an adjoining room for soups, fruits and ices; hot, cold and vapour baths.

As Clifton had still been in gestation when better-known thermal resorts, such as Bath, were at the height of their popularity, it was inevitable that attempts to capitalise on the eighteenth century vogue for congregating at watering places should have come later in Clifton than elsewhere. In fact, the fashion was nearing an end by the early nineteenth century, and it eventually became apparent that the new building had been constructed too late to realise its full potential. By the middle of the century, the Hotel was becoming outmoded, while the Assembly Rooms seemed to belong to another age. The latter were put up for sale, the rest of the building being converted into houses and shops.

The architectural authority, Ison, writing more recently, has attempted to describe the Assembly Rooms as they originally were:

> The Mall elevation, which is wholly built in dressed freestone, consists of a central block flanked by recessed wings. The central block (which is the least altered part of the design), is adorned with an engaged colonnade of six Ionic plain-shafted columns, rising from a low basement of rusticated arches, and embracing two storeys. The order consists of half-columns between the three-quarter columns that serve a return bay at each end. The inter columnisations are equal in width, and each contains one first and one second storey window. Those of the first storey have been altered but were plain originally, like those above them. The columns support the appropriate architrave, but in place of the orthodox frieze there is an attic-storey with five windows centred over those below. This attic is surmounted by a triangular pediment with a carved shield in its tympanum.

Recesses break each projecting wing into two bays that are equal in width but differ in plan. That nearest the centre is rectangular and has two windows to each storey, while the lateral bay is segmental and three windows wide. These wings are of equal height with the central block, and the rectangular windows of the three storeys were placed without architraves in a plain wall face that terminates with a frieze, cornice and parapet. The basement and first storey have been greatly altered, but the original low basement was arcaded to correspond with that of the central block, while between each bay was a lofty archway opening to a porch with steps rising to doorways in the first storey.

The rooms were planned as an open suite, the centrally-placed ballroom having an ante-recess in the middle of each long side. One opened through a glazed screen to a card room overlooking the Mall, while the other (now built up) led into the tea-room. The decorations were in a restrained Grecian style and the plasterwork has generally survived, but changing taste has left its dingy evidence to obscure the original colouring, which was carried out by Cornelius Dixon.

The most elaborate scheme is that of the ballroom, where engaged half-columns and pilasters divide the walls into bays and support a continuous entablature. A simple Corinthian order is used, one with moulded bases, plain shafts and capitals formed of acanthus and water-leaves modelled on those of the Tower-of-the-Winds portico. These columns and pilasters were originally marbled with Sienna shafts and statuary bases and capitals. Each long wall is formed into three bays by two widely spaced pairs of half-columns, each pair framing an arch-headed niche and supporting a projection of the entablature. The wide middle bay contains the arch-headed opening to the ante-recess, and in each end bay is a doorway, with a mahogany double door framed in a moulded architrave with a fluted frieze and cornice resting on consoles. The pilasters divide each end wall into three equal bays, each lateral one containing a shallow, arch-headed recess, while in the centre is a mirror of the same form placed above a chimney-piece with console-jambs. From above the entablature rises a deep cove that merges into the flat ceiling. Groined intersections break into this cove in the centre of each short side, and above the entablature projections on the long sides. A large saucer-domed skylight rises from a moulded surround in the ceiling's centre and the adjacent surfaces were originally painted to simulate coffers with moulded rosettes.

6

Purchase of Assembly Rooms and Royal Hotel

Having opened in in November 1811 as the Auriol Hotel and changed name five times in some forty years, the Royal Hotel (as it was finally known) was closed down and put on the market. It had outlived its purpose. The original owner, John Lewis Auriol, had leased the hotel to Mrs Mary Long in 1837 at an annual rent of £440, and on the expiry of this lease in 1851, a sale by auction was advertised.

The printed notice of sale, reproduced opposite, contains an exhaustive description of the building, the salient features being:

> Basement: Kitchens, Sculleries, Larder, Pantry and other Offices, Servants' Hall and two other Sitting Rooms, and extensive Cellaring with a Wine and Spirit Shop and a Court or Passage from the Lane behind; a Tap Room, Bar and Sitting and Lodging Rooms... opening upon Stable Lane (Waterloo Street).
>
> On the Ground Floor: two Ball Rooms... with small Dressing Room attached; large Coffee Room; Card Room and Billiard Room; three Sitting Rooms and two Bed Rooms; Waiters' Room and Pantry; Bar and Bar Parlour, with three other rooms used as Servants' Rooms.
>
> On the Drawing Room Floor: six Sitting Rooms, with twenty Bed Rooms and Dressing Rooms; on the Upper Floor two Sitting Rooms, and twenty-five Bed Rooms, with Bath and Bath Room.

PARTICULARS.

LOT 1.

A CAPITAL MESSUAGE,

BUILT FOR AND ALWAYS USED AS AN HOTEL,

ORIGINALLY CALLED

"THE AURIOL," afterwards "MANGEON'S HOTEL,"

AND FOR SOME TIME PAST KNOWN AS

THE ROYAL VICTORIA HOTEL,

Situate in The MALL,

And comprising Nos. 1 and 2, in *Mall Buildings*, at *Clifton*, within the city and county of *Bristol*, now in the occupation of Mrs. Mary Long, under Lease from John Lewis Auriol, Esquire, dated 11th November 1837, for 14 years, at the yearly rent of £440, payable quarterly.

This House is in length on the Front 110 Feet or thereabouts, and on the Back part next to Stable Lane, otherwise "Waterloo Street," 110 Feet or thereabouts, and in depth on the North-West side about 98 Feet, and on the South-East side about 94 Feet.

The House contains, on the Basement Story, large Kitchens, Sculleries, Larder, Pantry, and other Offices, Servants' Hall, and two other Sitting Rooms, and extensive Cellaring, with a Wine and Spirit Shop, and Sitting Rooms behind, under the South-East Wing, having Entrances from the Street in Front, and a Court or Passage from the Lane behind; a Tap Room, Bar, and Sitting and Lodging Rooms at the back part of the Building, and opening upon the Lane or Street there.

On the Ground Floor are two Ball Rooms, one 44 Feet in length by 26 Feet in depth; the other 29 Feet in length by 27½ Feet in depth, with small Dressing Room attached; large Coffee Room, 41 Feet in length by 28 Feet in depth; Card Room and Billiard Room; three Sitting Rooms and two Bed Rooms; Waiters' Room and Pantry; Bar and Bar Parlor, with three other Rooms, used as Servants' Rooms.

On the Drawing Room Floor are six Sitting Rooms, with twenty Bed Rooms, and Dressing Rooms; and on the Upper Floor are two Sitting Rooms, and twenty-five Bed Rooms, with Bath and Bath Room.

There are large Reservoirs for Spring Water, which is supplied from a Public Spring at Clifton, at an Annual Rent, and there are large Cisterns for Rain Water, which are well supplied from the extensive Roof.

The whole Building is in perfect condition and repair, and has been fitted up in an elegant manner at a very considerable expense.

The Premises in this Lot are charged with a certain Ground Rent of £45. 16*s*., as specified in the annexed Conditions of Sale; and this Lot is sold subject also to an Annual charge of £2. for Sewers' Rate.

The Lease of this Lot includes a Room taken from the First Floor of an adjoining House, being Lot 5 in the Particulars, and connected with the Hotel by a Passage between the two Buildings and the House, having afterwards been let by a separate Lease to the Tenant of the Hotel; a further addition was made by him to the Hotel, of the three other Rooms taken from the Upper Floor of the same House. The apportioned Rent for this Lot during the continuance of these Leases, is £420.

LOT 2.

A MESSUAGE, being No. 4, in *Mall Buildings, Clifton*, late in the occupation of the Rev. J. Taylor, as Tenant, and now void.

This House contains on the Basement Story, Housekeeper's Room and Pantry; two large Kitchens, with Oven and Dresser; Sculleries; several Beer and Wine Cellars and Pantries; Coal Cellar, &c., with two Courts behind.

On the Ground Floor are a large Dining Room, Parlor, Library, Breakfast Room, large China Pantry, and Water Closet.

> Large Reservoirs for Spring Water, supplied from a Public Spring at Clifton, at an Annual Rent, and large Cisterns for Rain Water supplied from the extensive Roof.
>
> The whole Building in perfect condition and repair fitted up in an elegant manner at a very considerable expense.

By the autumn of 1855 the building was still awaiting a new owner, when a scheme for its purchase was worked out and the following summary of intent was declared by the founder members of the club subsequently formed:

> That a capital of £7,000 be raised for this purpose in 140 shares of £50 each — the liability of each Shareholder extending only to the amount subscribed, as it is proposed the Company should be formed under the Limited Liabilities Act.
>
> The present Suite of Ball Rooms to be converted into promenade and reading rooms — the floor being lowered so as to give a better access to them.
>
> The Hotel either to be used as an Hotel or it may be converted into two shops, or otherwise altered as may be hereafter determined upon.
>
> The Tap to remain in its present state.
>
> The estimated Expense of purchasing the premises, of the conversion of a part into Shops and Baths — for decorating the reading room, painting and papering the Tap, Houses etc, including Law Expenses, Architect's fees etc, would not exceed £7,000.
>
> The Annual Income obtainable for the premises when altered is estimated at £500 a year with a probability of its increasing in a year or two.

Several interested parties, who had already enrolled as subscribers, met at Mr Burroughs' residence in West Mall on 29 November 1855, when it was decided that Mr Kempster be authorised to purchase the Hotel at £4,000. The offer was duly made and conditionally accepted, although Mr Wasbrough had collected no more than £3,500 from local subscribers. The draft contract was read and approved at a meeting on 9 February 1856, held this time in the former Assembly Rooms. It was resolved that subscriptions be deposited in the West of England and South Wales District Bank and that a mortgage be obtained to make up the shortfall of £500.

It was also unanimously resolved:

> That Trustees be appointed and that on the completion of the purchase the said premises shall be conveyed to them upon trust for the Shareholders.
>
> That contemporaneously with the Conveyance to the Trustees a Deed setting forth the Trusts on which the said premises are to be held shall be executed and that such Deed shall contain provisions for the management and conducting the said property, and the receiving and distributing the profits thereof. For the sale exchange and leasing of the same — with powers to raise if it shall be required on mortgage of the premises for the time being subject to the Trusts a sum not exceeding three thousand pounds inclusive of any monies which may be required to complete the purchase.

Finally, a Provisional Committee was appointed to oversee the preliminary arrangements. This included all the main founder members of the second Clifton Club: Mr Burroughs, Mr Kempster, Mr Colthurst, Reverend Benjamin Winthrop, Dr Symonds, Mr George Cooke, Mr Walwyn, Mr Lane, Mr Edward Clark, Mr Tovey and Mr Cooper. The Provisional Secretary was to be Mr Wasbrough.

At a meeting held on 22 May 1856, it was resolved that the purchase should go ahead, and the Secretary was empowered to offer £50 for the ground rent. One month later, it was announced that the purchase of the property had been effected. and the money handed over with £12.1.2d interest.

As representatives of the shareholders who now owned the former Royal Hotel and Assembly Rooms, the Committee was faced by decisions as to how this imposing building should be adapted to suit its new purpose — and indeed, what this new purpose should be. It seems that initially some kind of community centre was envisaged:

> The main object in purchasing the Hotel and adjoining premises is to appropriate them to such purposes as shall be most beneficial to the interests of Clifton, and especially that a portion should be appropriated for Public Rooms.

A general brief was drawn up by three of the subscribing gentlemen. After their suggestions of setting up communal baths and a family hotel had been dismissed, the following was agreed:

> The principal object in purchasing these premises being the establishment of public rooms... the Sub Committee recommend that the centre portion of the building comprising the three rooms formerly used as the Clifton Assembly Rooms, should be appropriated for that purpose, and that in connection therewith a shop should be fitted up for and rented to a Stationer, who might take the management of such rooms under the supervision of the Committee... A portion of the premises over the Assembly Rooms may be set apart as a residence.

A dozen well-known local architects were invited to participate in a competition to convert the premises. As an incentive, there were to be prizes of twenty, fifteen and ten guineas for the winner and runners-up. Six of the architects responded, using pseudonyms, and submitted plans based on the following brief:

> The floors of the Assembly Rooms to be kept at their present levels.
>
> The back room to be converted into a Billiard Room.
>
> The Tap to be divided off from the rest of the buildings for a respectable tavern.
>
> The site of the Coffee Room to be converted into a shop for a Bookseller and Stationer.
>
> The access to the Subscription Rooms to be improved and rendered easy.

> The remaining portion of the premises to be left to the discretion of the Architects whether for shops or otherwise, except that no portion is to be converted into an Hotel or Public Baths.
>
> That in the plans regard must be had to the preservation of the Cellars... and to the upper portion of the front elevation, and to a moderate outlay of money.
>
> That the estimated expenditure for the several portions of the premises should accompany the plans.

When the Committee met again on 27 June 1856, Mr Medland (an architect from Gloucester) was in attendance to explain the details of the six plans submitted for the conversion. Those selected were Palmam Qui Meruit Ferat, Trust and Try and Cliftoniensis in that order. The sealed envelopes having been opened, it was revealed that Mr J H Hirst had won the first prize of twenty guineas. (Of the few surviving buildings designed by this competent architect, the exterior of the Royal West of England Academy is probably the most striking; he was also responsible for St Peter's Church in Harrogate, where his practice was based.)

The Committee resolved to start the more urgent alterations at once, with Mr Hirst superintending the work. This was to be financed by a loan from Mr Bates with interest of 5% whatever the amount required, on the security of the Deeds, which he would hold. It is unfortunate that all the drawings submitted by the competing architects have been lost; however, detailed specifications of the intended works were minuted on 28 June 1856 and bound as Book III , which is currently kept at Bristol Records Office.

The winning entry and the submission awarded fifteen guineas had a number of features in common: the upper part of the front elevation remained untouched, the original entrance was retained as access to the public rooms, the part of the hotel which faced Waterloo Street was converted into shops, while the front was converted into shops with mezzanine storeys and the billiard room was lighted from above.

The following extract from Hirst's letter describes the alterations:

First: Cellars The whole block remains untouched as the proprietors desired.

Second: Public Rooms etc In providing the Public Rooms, all the old walls are retained. The following are the principal alterations made. A wide Entrance Porch and Corridor is provided at the side of the new Bookseller's Shop. This Corridor, of which a feature has been made, is shown divided from the Bookseller's Shop by Arches standing on light coupled columns, which arrangement it is believed would be highly advantageous in case the Occupier of the Shop should be also Superintendent and Manager of the Public Rooms. The arched openings might, if thought desirable, be filled with glass, still allowing the Superintendent that constant supervision so desirable without of necessity leaving his business, and at the same time securing a better light to the Entrance than would be otherwise possible.

An ascent of a few steps to the left leads to a small Vestibule from which both the large rooms are entered. This short staircase is well-lighted by borrowed lights from the Morning Room facing the Mall. Across the Vestibule are the Hat and Cloak Rooms similarly lighted. The Morning Room remains as at present. Glass doors will divide it from the Vestibule. Folding glass doors are also placed between the Vestibule and large Reading Room. In this room it is proposed to open the large dome light by removing entirely the shaft and bringing the glass skylight to the Ceiling level as shewn on the back elevation. Very good light and much increased effect will be thus obtained. Beyond repairs and decorations, no other alterations are intended. The doors right and left on the East side give access to the Lavatories, WC's etc and also to the Billiard Room, the present entrance being closed. The Billiard Room is that facing the Back Street and has a separate access from the Street. As the various rooms over are not conveniently situated to attach to other lettings, it is proposed to do away with them and make use of the materials. Several other advantages also arise. The Billiard Room can be increased in height, improved in proportion and what is of still greater importance sufficiently lighted and ventilated together with the conveniences from above. A further advantage is the securing considerably increased light and air at the Dome of the Reading Room.

From the lobby north of the Billiard Room, access may be had to two large rooms suitable for Refreshment and separate Smoking Rooms, shewn as portions of the adjoining letting.

Third: Hotel etc Very slight alterations are required in the arrangement of this portion. A new Staircase and new front (to prevent a nuisance corner) being almost all that is required.

Fourth and Fifth: Bookseller's and adjoining shop In providing these shops, advantage has been taken of the great height available in consequence of preserving the upper portion of the Building, to form shops of as noble proportions as the space permitted. In the elevation submitted, the whole facade of public rooms with the shops etc both above and below has been shewn coloured so as to give as exact an idea as possible of the effect when finished. It will be remarked that a large separate Entrance is provided for the public portion as well as separate and distinct Entrances to the Houses attached to the Shops. Over these latter Entrances mezzanine storeys have been contrived so that the great height may not be wasted, but on the contrary increased accommodation found for a Library or any other purpose. To obtain access to this mezzanine is a central iron column and spiral staircase with gallery. This iron column is necessary for constructive purposes, viz: to support the present division wall from thence to the top of the house, and would otherwise be a great eyesore. The purple and green colourings shew what house accommodation is attached to each of these lettings. To the Bookseller's Shop are added all those rooms on the Upper Floors over the public rooms not required for public purposes — these are converted into Kitchens, Sitting and Bedrooms with but slight additions or alterations.

The present staircase next the area is retained, fourteen steps placed in the passage leading to its foot. Leading from the first pair to the Upper Floors a new staircase is shewn in a more convenient position. The Lower Shop has a new staircase throughout, or rather an old one with considerable additions. To form these shops, new dwarf walls to take the floors will be required and to form separate private entrances, a new party wall from foundation to roof. The shop fronts will of course be entirely new with iron ornamental columns, plate glass etc as shewn. The form of the shop windows, part of a polygon on plan, is recommended as exceedingly effective in execution and further in this case peculiarly well adapted to the shape of the present buildings, which has a circular projection nearly corresponding in size with the bay. This projection would be best supported by means of columns arranged as shewn.

The Sixth portion is laid out as Shops with dwellings attached, it being the opinion of the Author of this design that no method more likely to pay the interest of any outlay could be suggested, arranged as shewn, these four Shops and Dwellings would cost about one hundred and fifty pounds each, and it is thought would provide a rental of from thirty to thirty-five pounds per annum each.

The estimated cost of the additions and alterations enumerated under the five first headings, including plain painting and putting in tenantable repair is nineteen hundred pounds.

7

Alterations and Refurbishment

No time was lost in adapting Clifton's most prestigious building to suit the requirements of the select group of gentlemen whose ultimate aim was to resurrect the original Clifton Club. It may be assumed that they had been members of that Club and witnessed its gradual decline. As gentlemen of means who were involved in the business world, they had finance, time and experience to devote to the creation of new and superior premises. A home-from-home would thus be provided, where they could regularly escape from the stress of family life.

At the Club they would challenge each other to games of billiards and generally enjoy themselves without standing on ceremony.

Although there had at first been some philanthropic notions of converting the building into a kind of civic centre, these were soon eclipsed by the group's enthusiasm for re-establishing the former Club on such splendid premises. The Assembly Rooms, which had once been the most public venue in Clifton, were about to become the most private and exclusive.

During the summer of 1856, Mr Hirst's plans were discussed by the Sub-Committee for superintending the alterations. They began with the conversion of the coffee room (now occupied by the Halifax, at No 20 The Mall) to house a bookseller's shop, which would provide newspapers and periodicals at a discount. A cellar would be excavated beneath this, a kitchen created in the space at the rear, and the four rooms above were to be connected with it by a new staircase. Thus a shop with living accommodation was created for the colourful Mr Mardon, the first Manager of the Club, of whom more will be related in due course.

As it seemed logical to build the adjoining shops at the same time, their undulating stone fronts with mahogany doors and windows also date from 1856. The shop fronts on Waterloo Street, however, were constructed of freestone.

It is worth noting that the proposed alterations included the removal of the main access staircase leading to the first floor, which commenced immediately inside the front door. There were in fact four such staircases along the total frontage of the building, all mounting directly from the pavement. Evidence of this design feature exists in plates surviving from the Clifton Hotel, some of which have been preserved and now hang on the walls in the Club bar. Once the main access staircase had been removed, it was replaced by two others which mounted to first floor level from the end of the new passageway. Like the bookshop floor, this was to be laid with coloured encaustic tiles which were fashionable in residential developments of the period — but exceeded the budget, necessitating a £20 contribution from Mr Mardon.

Mr Hirst was expected to act as quasi-builder, obtain

quotations from tradesmen, co-ordinate their activities on site and agree payments, just as Greenway, the original architect, had done. When his plans for the alterations had been confirmed, some four dozen letters were sent out requesting estimates from a number of masons, carpenters, plasterers, painters, tilers, plumbers, glaziers, bellhangers, iron founders and gas fitters. On 19 September 1856, at a General Meeting of Shareholders, the Building Committee was empowered to proceed with the works to a maximum of £3,000, excluding decorating and painting. To cover this outlay, the property was eventually mortgaged to the Rev H Barker for £4,000 at 4½%. In addition, a prospectus was issued locally with the aim of attracting more shareholders to the original nucleus.

Alterations to the building commenced under the appointed Clerk of Works, Mr Thomas Norman, whose salary was thirty shillings a week. Within days, the ownership of a cellar (adjacent to the present wine cellar) was called into question, when it was claimed by Mr Rowley of No 3 Mall Buildings. A firm of Solicitors, Messrs Stanley & Wasbrough, was requested to write and threaten legal proceedings; however, they were also authorised to offer to purchase No 3 should Mr Rowley prove difficult. It cannot be firmly established that the Club lost its case, but it is a fact that the cellar concerned remains an underground extension of the adjoining shop which became No 24 The Mall.

It was easier to appease another neighbour when over-zealous workmen accidentally knocked through a party wall. As the minutes record:

> A letter was read from Mrs Myers complaining of her apartments adjoining the hotel having been broken open by the workmen... by which she had been much inconvenienced and prevented from her daily employment for three days, and asking some assistance in consequence. Ordered that a sovereign should be given her.

In spite of such setbacks, the alterations were rapidly carried out. Only four months after the start of structural works, as rolls of patterned wallpaper were being hung, the architect was deciding on colour schemes and selecting the furniture and soft furnishings. Carpets were ordered from Messrs Birds, who were willing to supply and lay patterned carpets with borders at a mere 4/8d per square yard. It was normal to make the carpets smaller than the rooms for which they were intended, leaving a border of stained wood. The large reading room and the refreshment room were to be covered with 'a strong Brussels carpet of a mixed Turkey pattern', while a central Turkey carpet was to be surrounded by a patterned floor covering in the front room. Messrs Birds were also the chosen supplier of 'trap rods with ornamental ends' to hang their curtains which, at 8/6d per yard, seem expensive in relation to the carpets.

Meanwhile, Mr Laverton was constructing thirty chairs for the premises, half of which were to have spring stuffed seats 'and the other half to be stuffed with best horsehair and to be covered with Utrecht velvet'. Obviously heavy, they would be provided with special castors. Another two chairs were specially ordered from Liverpool, to resemble the chairs which had so impressed the Secretary on visiting the Athenæum Club there. These are still in use at the Clifton Club today.

To complete the furniture, Mr Board received a substantial order for hand-crafted settees and leather-covered tables. Two outsize tables (twelve foot by six) which were intended for the large room, have been serving the members ever since. The front room seems to have been most carefully furnished, with velvet-covered settees on each side of the two fireplaces and another, centrally placed on the Turkey carpet. Leather-covered writing tables were placed within reach, while semi-circular tables to match were decoratively positioned between the windows overlooking the Mall, at which outside Venetian blinds were fixed. (The settees, intended to match Mr Lavington's chairs, were upholstered in velvet which cost as much as 14/6d per square foot.) The egg moulding of the cornice had been carefully gilded, in order to enhance this elegant picture, which was reflected in large oblong mirrors fixed above the fireplaces at either end of the front room. As a finishing touch, different timepieces were selected from the catalogues of Mr Cordeux, the clockmaker, whose establishment on the site of the present-day 'Quadrant' seemed a permanent feature of Clifton.

The mirrors were repeated above the end fireplaces in the centre room, each of which was flanked by two similar settees, with writing tables conveniently situated nearby. As unrestricted smoking was to be permitted in the large billiard room, four settees upholstered in American leather (at 12/6d per square foot) were ordered for each side of the two fireplaces there. Presumably the leather was more resistant to cigar ash, which sometimes missed the ash bowls. It may also have been for this reason that the floor covering was quickly replaced by more durable India matting. To exclude drifting smoke from the reading and refreshment rooms, the architect was requested to have two sets of double doors installed.

By the summer of 1857, the refurbished premises were beginning to look almost too elegant. As an afterthought, covers in Bronn Holland were ordered for all the seating. Another afterthought resulted in the creation of a second billiard room; a second billiard table and more leather-upholstered settees were consequently added to the furniture lists. At the completion date, 25 September 1857, the former Assembly Rooms were finally ready for their new patrons — who, unable to wait so long, had already enthusiastically laid claim to the premises two months earlier!

At the second AGM of the Association, held in March 1858, it was announced that, although additional building works had been required, the whole project had now reached a gratifying conclusion:

> From the opening of the Rooms, a success has attended the undertaking far surpassing the anticipations of its promoters so that it was found necessary to make several additions... materially increasing the comfort and convenience of the establishment. Amongst these the Committee would refer to the creation of a new and separate entrance into the Billiard Rooms directly from the Vestibule, the only access to them before being through the Large Reading Room, which created a source of annoyance to the frequenters of that Room by the continual passing and repassing.

In keeping with its refurbished splendour, the new venture was officially known as the Clifton Subscription Rooms Association. However, as this was quite a mouthful, people tended to refer more simply to 'the Clifton Club', as they had done with its predecessor near Birdcage Walk.

Step inside the Clifton Club as it is today

The Hallway and Entrance

Originally, the mirrored wall on the left was clear glass so that the manager of the adjoining bookshop, who also managed the Club, could keep an eye on people entering and leaving the building

Below – the Porter's Lodge, to the right of the hallway

Rooflight over the main staircase

Entrance to St Andrew's churchyard and Birdcage Walk, a favourite route followed by members of the original Club

A stone outline and commemorative tablet is all that is remains of St Andrew's Church which was close to the site of the first Clifton Club

The tiny parish church that was originally built to serve Clifton's sparse rural population, had been demolished by 1822 and reconstructed to hold 2,000 people. This enlarged church was destroyed by fire during the Second World War

Francis Greenway – the only known forger to be immortalised in this fashion (detail from an Australian $10 banknote)

Francis Greenway was finally acknowledged in the United Kingdom too, when this plaque appeared outside the present Clifton Club premises, the only surviving building designed by the architect in this country

This painting of a scene in the courtyard of Newgate Prison, Bristol, is attributed to Francis Greenway, who spent many months there awaiting trial for forgery

St James' Church in 1836, one of many buildings designed by Greenway for Sydney, it is now dwarfed by city skyscrapers

Both oil painting and hand-coloured lithograph are reproduced by courtesy of the Mitchell Library, Sydney

The Billiard Room has hardly changed since the nineteenth century

Carved wooden fireplace bearing the Club monogram (top left)
and the date, 1889 (top right)

The Bridge Room

Stained glass windows prevent any distraction from the street below, which was formerly known as Stable Lane

The Centenary Room, used as a ballroom before 1855, when the present Club premises were used to host major social events in Clifton, as illustrated in the painting that hangs above the fireplace

Vista from the Centenary Room to windows in the façade which overlook the Mall Gardens

8

Nineteenth Century Building Services

Water Supply

When the original subscribers first decided to purchase the Royal Hotel in 1855, one of their proposals was to convert part of it into baths for public use. Today the word 'baths' conjures up a picture of minimally clad people swimming lengths for exercise or diversion. In the nineteenth century, however, such an establishment was strictly functional, patronised by people who found it difficult to maintain personal hygiene at home due to the general lack of water. 'Baths' would have been more of a communal bathroom.

Although a very small proportion of houses actually received water through pipes as a result of private experimental schemes, the traditional method of collecting water from conduits, pumps or wells was most commonly used. Those who could afford to pay one penny a bucketful had the commodity delivered to their door by perambulating water-sellers. In this respect, very little had changed since the middle ages. Despite the abundance of water available in Bristol, access to an unpolluted supply was limited. In 1840 a Government Commission had issued a report on the city and its water supply from which the following extract is taken:

> Viewed as a sanitary question, there are few if any large towns in England in which the supply of water is so inadequate as at Bristol. The labour and consequent expense attached to the system of obtaining a supply of water from the draw wells or pumps engenders filthy habits directly acting upon the health, and indirectly upon the morals, of the people... The labour of fetching water leads to a very sparing use of it.

The following year, the Merchant Venturers attempted to improve these insanitary conditions by applying to Parliament for permission to supply Clifton and nearby districts from the two Hot Well springs on the banks of the Avon, which were said to produce at least 94,000 gallons daily. The owners of the new Clifton springs managed to prevent the success of this enterprise, however, and maintained a monopoly in supplying water to Clifton residents until 1847. At this date the Bristol Waterworks Company, sanctioned by Parliament, commenced the supply of clean water to the twenty-two thousand households of Bristol. The Company had purchased the three Clifton springs (Sion, Richmond and Buckingham) for a total of £20,646 and in addition had reimbursed the Merchant Venturers for costs incurred when several miles of cast iron pipes were prematurely laid in Clifton. A further sixty-five miles of pipe had been laid throughout the city by Bristol Water Works, who also built three reservoirs for storage of the 'pure and wholesome water' which the company guaranteed to supply. It flowed into Bristol at the rate of some four million gallons daily. In May 1848 the Bristol Mirror reported that:

> The supply of pure and translucent water which has recently been introduced to our city from the heights of Mendip and Barrow has been profuse in the extreme.

From the record of water rates, which were paid in advance quarterly, it is clear that only two per cent of homes in Bristol were receiving piped water by 1848. It would obviously have taken years for the new company to include every household in the network. In the meanwhile, however, public baths and wash houses were established for those who had no running water at home — the majority. This was a civilised refinement which had not been seen in England since the time of the Romans! The idea of creating communal washing facilities was evidently fashionable in the 1850s, so that it would have been natural to suggest such a use for the Assembly Rooms and Royal Hotel.

It would seem that the building had been well supplied with piped water since its opening as the Auriol in 1811, presumably from the Sion spring. Situated on rocks above Hotwells, this had been discovered during the late eighteenth century by a solicitor, who was boring for a domestic water supply. The quantities of hot water yielded daily — 34,000 gallons — greatly exceeded his expectations! He built a pump house for the benefit of visitors to the spa, who were thus spared the laborious descent to the original pump house constructed on a promontory in Hotwells. To make better use of the abundant daily flow, pipes were laid from the spring into houses in Prince's Place.

The supply of piped water began in 1800 and a decade later most houses in the south west of Clifton were included. The Assembly Rooms and Hotel would certainly have been among them. In fact, 'hot, cold and vapour baths' were offered in the newly-built hotel for the benefit of visitors to the spa, which would suggest that a plentiful supply of natural hot water was available there. The spring water could also be stored in reservoirs which existed in the basement.

Not only did Greenway's building on the Mall receive piped water from the start, but like many of the older properties in Clifton, it was provided with an underground back-up tank to store rainwater collected from the extensive roofs. In this way it was well ahead of the times and sufficiently provided with water to cope with the modest demands of users in the kitchens and bathrooms. When Mr Hirst carried out his refurbishment in 1856, the large rainwater cistern was not included in arrangements for a water supply, which indicates that adequate amounts were already being piped into the building from Sion spring. The rainwater from the roof was diverted and pipes leading to the cistern were obviously removed. During the following decade, the forgotten cistern was re-discovered and the Committee was informed of its existence in 1864:

> Mr Hartland, the Manager, having reported that a soft water cistern 26 feet long, 12 feet broad and 6½ feet deep had been ascertained to be under the Club premises, and that at present there was 3 feet of water therein. Mr Maggs' estimate, amounting to £24.10.0d, for finding and laying pipes to convey the water from the roof of the club premises into the said cistern, to find and fix a new and proper lifting pump to force the water from soft water cistern to tank on roof and to perform all the necessary work appertaining thereto... was accepted.

As the minutes contain no further reference to this cistern, which still exists in the cellars beneath the building, we can only assume that its original function was successfully restored for some years. It is probable that the collection of rainwater was discontinued in 1869 when the Committee resolved 'that the Water Works Company be instructed to lay on their water to supply the Club at the rate of £2.16.6d per quarter'. Once again, water from the roof was diverted and pipes to the rainwater cistern were removed as the Club joined other subscribers to the local water board.

Lighting

Where lighting was concerned, it is likely that the Assembly Rooms and Hotel were illuminated by large quantities of tallow candles during the early years, as gas lighting was still in its infancy. A few isolated pioneers had experimented with illumination by means of gas during the eighteenth century, and Greenway must have been aware of the revolutionary new concept. The first gasworks were set up in London where, in 1807, Pall Mall was unique in England for its gas lighting. This was four years before the opening of the Hotel and Assembly Rooms in the Mall at Clifton, when the unfortunate architect was struggling with financial problems and may not have been too concerned about the virtues of gas illumination.

Since classical times rushlights, tallow candles and oil lamps had been the only source of artificial light, providing restricted illumination by means of a flickering flame. During the early part of the nineteenth century there were rapid developments in the use of gas for lighting purposes, coinciding with the invention of the match in 1827. While most people retained the old methods of lighting, gas represented a major technological advance in the illumination of public buildings and the homes of the wealthy. For the first time in European history, it became possible to light a complete room by means of a pipe through which gas was fed and ignited at a bracket on the wall. The shape of the flame was dictated by a variety of burners, culminating in the Argand burner which was invented as early as 1820.

Bearing in mind that gas lighting was not installed in the House of Commons until 1852, it cannot be assumed that the Hotel would have adopted the new system as soon as commercial gas became available in Bristol, especially as the initial success of the building had waned rapidly, bringing problems of a financial nature. When the building was sold to Clifton Club subscribers in 1856, it is probable that gas lighting was partially installed.

By the middle of the century, lighting had become essential, both indoors and in the streets — where previously there had been no illumination. Gas fitters were among the tradesmen approached for the refurbishment of the building in the Mall and it is significant that only one of these had time to prepare an estimate. Meanwhile, Mr Hirst was despatched to London 'for the purpose of inspecting the different modes of lighting adopted in the Club Houses and public edifices'. He would have travelled by the relatively new railway, which was far more convenient than the traditional horse-drawn alternative. On his return, it was decided to illuminate the front room by means of two wall lights at either end and a central gasolier with eight mantles. The large centre room and the billiard room were to be similarly illuminated, all under the direction of Mr Strode of London, who would personally visit Clifton while the works were in progress to instruct the gas-fitter. One of the principal lighting and ventilation firms in England, Messrs Strode & Co were internationally known for their illumination of theatres and well qualified to light the former ballroom at the Clifton Club.

However, there were certain disadvantages with this new form of lighting: as well as being expensive, it had limited scope, giving only a general light, casting shadows at ground level and consuming mantles which needed continual replacement. For a more intense source of light, it was still necessary to resort to the candle or oil lamp which had been in common use for many centuries. There were also incidental drawbacks with gas lighting. The whitewashed plaster above a gas bracket appeared to be in frequent need of redecoration, due to deposits of soot, while the perennial problem of ventilation was certainly increased by gas lights. It was necessary to allow heat and fumes to escape at ceiling level above the gasoliers, which meant that an equal amount of cold air would enter the room by way of compensation. As well as replacing oxygen consumed by the flames this exacerbated the draughts, of which frequent complaint is made in the minutes. The larger the room and its source of light, the stronger would be the currents of cold air. Theatres, for example, were particularly draughty places and this was deplored by an article of 1870 in *The Builder*:

> If managers knew how many persons stay away from theatres because of the difficulty of avoiding cold and stiff neck, they would make the attempt to lessen the draughts which blow away money.

On the other hand, gas proved very useful for the external illuminations which became customary when royal occasions were celebrated. A design could be carried out in gas jets and colour was introduced by the burning of ground chemicals. The façade of the Club building was lit up in accordance with a selected design to mark the marriage of the Prince of Wales in 1863. Having paid a sum of £30 for the installation and subsequent removal of fittings, the Committee was displeased to note that the façade had been slightly damaged. Queen Victoria's Jubilee in 1887 was another occasion to be marked, and the façade was again fitted up and illuminated for the celebrations. For the Queen's final visit to Bristol in the last year of the century, neighbours contributed to a fund for illuminations in the Mall Gardens.

During the first decades of occupation by the Clifton Club, the gas lighting system installed in the building on the Mall was maintained and occasionally embellished with new gasoliers. (This Victorian word hardly overtaxes the imagination, since the appliance would have had much the same structure as a chandelier.) Towards the end of the century the introduction of incandescent gas burners gave a new lease of life to this form of lighting. Always abreast of the times, the Clifton Club Committee set about upgrading their existing gas lights with incandescent burners.

The rival invention of electricity was some decades behind gas. The Clifton Club had its very first experience of an electrical circuit in the 1880s with the bell system used to summon servants. It worked well as long as the wiring was not displaced by moving of carpets, which would seem to

indicate a rather superficial installation.

Various developments in electrical lighting were made from the 1850s onwards, but it was not until the 1880s that the final breakthrough came with the use of the filament lamp invented by Edison. The proprietors of the Clifton Club were among the first to realise the advantages of using electricity for lighting. The system seemed cleaner and more reliable than gas. Through flexible distribution wiring and the simple manipulation of a switch, a brighter light was instantly obtained. And lamps were a great improvement on mantles.

Gas as a form of energy held its own in the kitchen, however, where the gas stove remained unchallenged, having replaced the old range decades before. In 1888, in honour of the Queen's Jubilee, the Committee decided to spend the sum of £5 on yet another gas stove. There was a slight disadvantage in using both types of energy: the bills issued by the Bristol Gas Company, based in Canons Marsh, no longer qualified for a reduction of two pence per 1,000 cubic feet as amounts used annually fell just below the requisite million cubic feet in 1894.

Until 1894, the Clifton Club building had been exclusively gas-lit, but in that year electrical circuits were installed in certain rooms. Both forms of lighting were in use until the turn of the century, when electroliers suspended from the ceilings began to out-number the gasoliers, which had replaced the candle-burning chandeliers, and gas finally gave way to electricity where lighting was concerned.

9

Public Rooms, Family Rooms, Gentlemen's Club

When the main body of the Royal Hotel was purchased in 1856, the principal intention was to benefit Clifton through the establishment of public rooms. Older people could remember with nostalgia the elegant social gatherings which had taken place on the site — after all, these were the former Assembly Rooms, where all local Balls had been held for almost half a century. With this association in mind, the architect designed a Ladies Room with velvet-covered chimney piece, and ladies were to be seen in the Front Room, where the telegram stand was placed so that they might not be excluded from reading the telegraphic despatches.

Admission soon became more formal and restricted. In 1859, almost two years after the opening of the Subscription Rooms, an Extraordinary General Meeting was called to set up regulations regarding family membership.

> 1. That every Shareholder shall have free admission... and for each additional share he may hold, he shall also have the privilege of admitting his wife or a son residing with him and not under the age of seventeen years at a yearly subscription of half a guinea.
>
> 2. That the yearly subscription for gentlemen shall be two guineas. That the yearly subscription for ladies shall be one guinea... And that each yearly Subscriber may have the

> privilege of obtaining family tickets to admit three, being his wife or sons residing with him not under the age of seventeen years, upon the additional payment for one year of two guineas.

During 1859 areas of the premises patronised by gentlemen were extended. A 'new and commodious Smoking Room' was established, to which ladies would not have access. Youths were definitely excluded as from 1860; except for young commissioned officers, it was decreed that no person under twenty-one years of age should be admitted.

Twenty years after the Subscription Rooms were inaugurated, legal mayhem was caused when an emigrating member transferred his share to a lady. Since ladies were no longer welcome as subscribers or even guests, the Club Solicitors proposed that the recipient should be regarded as a trustee only and immediately transfer this share 'to any member to be approved of by the Committee'.

Imperceptibly, the public rooms had become a gentlemen's club, providing a refuge from the formality of mixed company, a place where members might spend their leisure hours in pleasant relaxation with their own kind. But there were still limits to be observed: any member who relaxed to the extent of putting his feet up was likely to receive an official reprimand, 'calling his attention to the notice requesting members not to put their feet on the chairs, sofas or other furniture of the Club'.

Curt notices of this nature and admonishing letters from the Secretary seemed to keep the Club running fairly smoothly. 'SILENCE IS REQUESTED' hung on the wall in the front room. A list of those members whose subscriptions were still pending was posted in the Reading Room at the start of each year. This must have been taken quite seriously by respectable Victorians for whom a bouncing cheque was scandalous and insolvency a social crime. Those rare members who were declared bankrupt were instantly expelled from the Club.

Although strict with regular members, the Committee kept up an unwavering public image of hospitality to professional groups who might be temporarily convening in Bristol. All were generously invited to become honorary members during their stay. This included members of the British Medical Association, the Incorporated Law Society, the Association of Chambers of Commerce, the Royal Sanitary Institute, Old Cliftonians during Commem week, and many more. Officers of regiments stationed at Horfield Barracks were invited on the same basis. Such frequent transfusions of outsiders prevented the Club from becoming too insular. To further broaden horizons, visitors from overseas were also welcomed as honorary members — for instance the Captain and crew of the United States ship *Enterprise* in 1889, and later the itinerant Mayor of Toowoomba, Queensland!

The public-spirited Committee was also willing to host important local meetings on the premises, which became a venue for Clifton Archery Club and Clifton Improvement Society. On 16 May 1860, the Mayor of Bristol and some gentlemen of Clifton held a historic meeting in one of the Club rooms 'for the purpose of considering the propriety of establishing a College at Clifton for the education of the Sons of Gentlemen'. At this meeting the concept of Clifton College (informally discussed at Mr Wasbrough's house the previous month) was officially recognised. Decisions taken at the meeting resulted in the building of the new school, which was opened two and a half years later.

In 1865, shortly after the inauguration of the Suspension Bridge, the transformation of Leigh Woods to a public recreation ground was envisaged, and the display of plans by an eminent landscape gardener was authorised on the Club premises. Curiously, the huge project of the Suspension Bridge, so close at hand, seems not to have impinged on the Committee in any way, as it is simply never mentioned in the Club minutes. Abandoned through lack of finance, the piers on each side of the Gorge had remained unconnected and it was many years before the bridge was actually finished. We can only assume that Clifton residents had lost interest in these 'monuments to failure', as the piers had been known.

Occasionally subscriptions were opened at the Club for humanitarian reasons, notably the Indian Famine Relief Fund in 1897. The Prince of Wales' National War Relief Fund in 1914 was also well patronised. When the worst floods for two centuries occurred nearer home in the spring of 1889, the shocked members hurriedly collected items of used clothing for victims in the flooded districts of Bristol. On a less disastrous note, the coronation gift to King George V from 'Georges in the British Empire' included a contribution from the Clifton Club, collected from any members bearing this name in 1910. And the national testimonial to W G Grace included donations from members of the Clifton Club, where at one time the famous cricketer had himself been a member.

The generosity of members was also in evidence with regard to their own premises and the Secretary was frequently asked to send letters of thanks on behalf of the Committee. Mr Gilpin started the trend in the 1870s, when he presented three lounging and two armchairs for use in the smoking room. All kinds of gifts followed in due course, as diverse as silver-plated tankards, ivory billiard balls or a box of fish knives and forks. Pictures which were framed and hung on the walls included a painting of the Beaufort Hunt and an interesting panorama of Clifton in 1830. Mr Fripp presented two dishes of historic interest, showing the façade of the Clifton Club when the building was known as the Clifton Hotel. (These are currently displayed in the bar area.)

Personalised in this way, the premises became a home-from-home for gentlemen with time on their hands. By the 1860s, it was unthinkable that ladies should be admitted to this haven on the Mall where their husbands were able to catch up with the news, smoke the Club cigars and indulge a boyish instinct for game-playing. Chess had been thoughtfully provided by the Committee and backgammon was also available, but the main addiction for many of the members was billiards.

Billiards

A very adequate Billiard Room was an integral part of the premises, but no sooner had it been opened in 1857 than a second room for billiards was found to be necessary. This was an expensive hobby, with specially ordered hand-made tables and two markers on duty in each room to receive the hourly hire of 1/6d and keep the score. They would also play with unaccompanied members for a fee, and were adept at the games of Race and Pyramid Pool which were fashionable with billiard devotees. Occasionally there were problems with markers who were unable to account for all the proceeds of billiard games, while a few managed to offend members. The most repetitive problem, however, involved damage to the cloth, which was often cut by careless players on flinging down their cues or singed when hot ash fell from cigars. They were always required to pay for the repair and the regrettable incident was then registered for posterity by a long-suffering Secretary.

Billiard players paid an increased charge after dusk to cover the cost of gas lighting. As wall brackets gave only a background glow, additional gas lights were fixed above the billiard table. At the turn of the century further improvements were made to the illumination, with the addition of

> six new frames, shades and holders and six incandescent Bypass burners fitted with mica chimneys and draught screens to Upper Billiard Room table.

But shadows were inevitably cast where good visibility was essential. Soon afterwards, as electricity became established for lighting purposes, it was found that an electric light suspended above the billiard table was more convenient. After fifty years of gaslights, shadow-free tables were procured by changing to this method of illumination.

Cards

Although both cards and billiards had been played at the original Clifton Club founded in 1818, only billiards were provided for when the Assembly Rooms were adapted as a second venue for the Club in the 1850s. To remedy this oversight and accommodate the many card-playing members,

the creation of a card room was later proposed and carried by 57 to 29. When a new card room was announced as part of the alterations of 1860, this potential moral and legal issue was immediately seized upon by the ecclesiastical members, who demanded that a sub-committee should be formed. Its brief was to 'draw up a case respecting the introduction of cards into the Rooms' and submit this to a London barrister for an opinion.

Those who were against the proposed card room contended that it would be such a significant alteration to the Deed of Settlement that a majority of at least two-thirds would be required at two separate meetings. They also maintained that they had joined the Club on the understanding that cards were expressly excluded. Those in favour of a card room quoted the prospectus, which had promised members 'all the advantages of a London Club' — and such advantages obviously included card-playing.

The London counsel finally gave a lengthy but logical opinion, ending with the words: 'On the whole then, I am of the opinion that it is competent for the Committee alone to introduce cards'. The moralists could only abide by the judgment they had requested. Soon furniture was being purchased for the new card room and charges were established. Each player would pay one shilling to cover the price of a new pack of cards, while any additional pack would cost two shillings. The initial ruling was that no pack of cards could be used twice. As a competitive supplier was offering a dozen packs for fifteen shillings and used cards could be sold off for one-third of that price, some profit was to be anticipated for the Committee.

Whist, Dummy Whist and Piquet seem to have been the most popular games, while Coon Can was later added to the list. The new Card Room was clearly much frequented. By 1873 it had been moved down to the main area of the Club, while the Smoking Room was banished to the top of the building, where card-players had been discreetly housed before. Whether or not the moralists approved, card-playing seemed to have become an established pastime at the Club.

The relatively new game of Bridge probably appeared at the Clifton Club towards the end of Queen Victoria's reign. It had arrived in London in 1894 when the Portland Club, founded in 1816, is said to have hosted the very first game of Bridge to be played in this country. Like certain other games, it was nurtured in gentlemen's clubs before being introduced to genteel circles.

Golf

Physical, outdoor energy was required for golf, the game which, during the second half of the nineteenth century, began to attract respectable middle-class citizens in this country. At the start of the century, there had only been a single golf course in England. Others gradually appeared, one of which was a municipal nine-hole course on Durdham Downs (between Blackboy Hill and Ladies Mile), where golfing enthusiasts from the Club were often to be found in the daytime.

When the Subscription Rooms had been running for thirty years, golf was still a very exclusive sport, with fewer than two hundred courses in the whole country. By 1896,

however, there were 1,400 courses in England, including the new Bristol & Clifton Golf Course, founded in 1891 by some of those confirmed golfers who had been joint members of the Clifton Downs Golf Club and the Clifton Club. These gentlemen, who called themselves the Leatherjackets, were able to purchase their equipment from a shop run by a former coach to Clifton College, Mr James Dryland. From the point of view of Clifton Club members, this was most appropriately located, being on the corner of Caledonia Place. The trip to Failand, however, was a lengthy one. The Suspension Bridge helped to shorten the route of course, and any golfers travelling by horse-drawn carriage were issued with season tickets for just five shillings. Their main expense was the subscription to the Golf Club, one guinea per annum.

The Leatherjackets always held their annual dinner at the Clifton Club. The link between the Clifton Club and the Golf Club was probably strongest while Mr Sleaman was Secretary to both establishments.

10

The Reading Rooms

It is impossible to trace the original function of each room on the Club premises, as these were continually being changed at the whim of the Committee. There was a smoking room, a card room, two billiard rooms, and two reading rooms, all of which moved around the building at frequent intervals. The reading rooms were of particular importance in times when the only form of media was the press. In order to cater for all tastes, far more newspapers were ordered than would be the case in any club today. The founder members drew up the following list of essential reading matter, to be delivered by Mr Mardon on a regular basis:

10 copies of *The Times*
1 *Morning Herald*
1 *Morning Post*
1 *Morning Chronicle*
2 *Daily News*
1 evening paper (early edition)
1 ditto (late edition)
1 *Examiner*
1 *Spectator*
1 *Illustrated London News*
1 *The Map*
1 *Railway Times*

1 *Athenæum*
1 *Guardian*
1 *Record*
1 *Naval & Military Gazette*
1 *United Service Gazette*
1 *Bell's Life*
1 *Punch*
1 *Indian News*
1 Bath paper

1 *Bristol Times*
1 *Mirror*
1 *Mercury*
1 *Advertiser*
1 *Clifton Chronicle*
1 *Bristol Gazette*
1 *Quarterly Review*
1 *Edinburgh Review*
1 *Westminster Review*
1 *Blackwood's Magazine*
1 *New Monthly Magazine*
1 *Bentley's Miscellany*
1 *United Service Magazine*
1 *Fraser's Magazine*
1 *Tait's Magazine*
1 *Dublin University Magazine*

Directories considered indispensable in any gentlemen's club were also ordered:

Army List
Navy List
Clergy List
Burke's Peerage
London Directory
Bristol Directory
Court Guide
East India Register

They were updated in 1864 when the list further included:

Suburban Directory
Oxford University Calendar
Cambridge University Calendar
Dod's Parliamentary Companion
Dod's Peerage
A good Dictionary

Half the newspapers were kept in the Centre Room, where a bookcase in the recess under the clock contained books such as the *Encyclopædia Britannica* (twenty-one volumes) and *Notes & Queries* (twelve volumes), specially purchased for £14 in all. Over the years, members occasionally donated leather-bound tomes; these were mainly military history and included twenty-three half-bound volumes of the *Wellington Despatches* by Colonel Gunwood, which the donor hoped would help form the nucleus of a library.

After a quarter of a century there was such a profusion of uncatalogued reading matter that a suggestion was made by Mr Tovey at the AGM of 1880:

> He thought that as there were very many books, reviews, periodicals etc, the accumulation of years, neglected and in confusion in another apartment, they might be bound and fitly placed, and thus form the foundation of a library that would be a source of pleasure and improvement to the members.

As a result of this appeal, a number of the periodicals were bound and retained and £50 was allocated towards the purchase of up-to-date books of reference:

Burke's Peerage
London Post Office Directory
Crockford's Clerical Directory
The Official Army List
India List
Parliamentary Companion
Statesman's Year Book
Landed Gentry
Medical Directory
Law List
Cambridge Calendar
Oxford Calendar

Circulating libraries were very popular at the time, notably that founded by Mr Mudie in 1842 which flourished as a national institution for almost a century. From the start the Committee had subscribed to the Clifton branch of Mudie's Library, which supplemented the available reading matter at the Club by loaning consignments of twenty books each month at an annual fee of ten guineas. Members were well aware that these might not be removed from the Club, but sometimes a book would be smuggled off the premises and finished at home. From time to time, severe notices appeared in the Reading Room, threatening that the library service would be discontinued if this practice persisted. Another fault of which certain members were guilty was the disturbing habit of reading aloud. Notices requesting silent reading were put up to discourage them. It was naturally assumed that members would treat the quantities of newspapers and magazines ordered with respect. Their unauthorised removal was also a problem, commented on at a Committee meeting in 1877:

> As the permission given to some of the members to take away certain papers etc on Saturday has been abused it was resolved that no member be allowed to take any papers or books out of the Club on any pretence whatever, according to rule No 17, and an intimation of this would be posted in the Rooms.

Eventually a stamp was purchased which would hopefully deter members from the unsanctioned borrowing which still occurred, and every paper or magazine bore on its cover 'Not to be Taken from this Room'.

It seemed that things were getting out of hand in the Reading Room when the 'mutilation of an illustrated paper' was reported to the Committee, and the following pained notice was posted on the wall:

> The Committee notice with regret that an illustrated paper has been defaced, and as this clearly cannot be the result of an accident, it is hoped it will not be repeated.

When pages were intentionally removed from magazines, a serious warning was issued:

> The Secretary was directed to put up a notice calling attention to rule 25, of which the above was a deliberate violation, rendering the offender liable to expulsion from the club.

Once the news was no longer fresh, however, huge piles of newspapers must have accumulated on the premises, with attendant disposal problems. Mr Massingham of Clifton Library finally agreed to buy old copies of the morning and weekly newspapers for twelve shillings per cwt, but he could only offer seven shillings for old pamphlets, magazines and waste paper. Newspapers were occasionally donated to the Sailors' Home or packaged up and sent abroad for the benefit of British troops, arriving many weeks after the date of issue, when news had become history.

11

Tenants on the Mall

From the outset, it was planned that the income of the new Club should partly consist of rent from peripheral areas of the newly purchased building, which would be converted to shops or small dwellings. The total rent anticipated each year was £500, to be made up as follows:

The Mall	Bookseller's	£150
	Grocer's shop	£130
	Fishmonger's	£35
Waterloo Street	Tavern	£70
	Four dwelling houses	£115

Bookseller's Shop

The first of the conversions carried out in 1856 was the shop and dwelling intended for a bookseller, on the site of the coffee room attached to the Royal Hotel (at No 20 The Mall today). It was hoped that the tenant would supply the Club with newspapers and periodicals at a discount. If he also filled the post of superintendent or manager of the Rooms, he would have an excellent vantage point and could inspect those entering the building through the glazed partition between the shop and the new entrance corridor.

Mr Edward Mardon agreed to manage the Rooms in conjunction with the bookseller's shop, where he would be assisted by his wife. He was evidently well-known to the shareholders, who held their first AGM at his residence in Regent Place. In the summer of 1856 he wrote to Mr Wasbrough confirming his arrangements to rent the new accommodation at £150 per annum and provide the following services:

> Making allowance for the privilege of having all the papers the day after publication and the magazines one month after publication, I can undertake to supply the Rooms as per enclosed list, find an attendant in livery whose whole time shall be devoted to the Rooms, keep the Accounts and become the Manager under a Committee which you will appoint for the sum of £230 per annum.

It soon became clear that the duties of a Superintendent of the Rooms had been greatly underestimated and could hardly be combined with running the adjoining bookshop. By the spring of 1858, Mr Mardon admitted that he was 'prepared to put an end to the present agreement at once and to adopt any course which the Committee might suggest'. He was quickly relieved of his appointment as Manager, being replaced as an interim measure by Mr Gall, who superintended the cleaning, received subscriptions and closed the Rooms at night.

Mr Mardon, obviously an impetuous and changeable character, thereupon decided to emigrate to Australia, on his own, and did so without delay. Here we lose track of him, as did his deserted wife. At this point Mrs Mardon's father, Mr Ashmead, became a tenant, renting the ground floor of one of the houses in Waterloo Street at £10 per annum, to contain a (horse-drawn) fire engine. As his son-in-law had 'broken his agreement and virtually abandoned his tenancy', Mr Ashmead wrote to the Committee on 1 September 1858, offering to take his place:

> Gentlemen
> I believe you are already aware that Mr Mardon has left Clifton for Australia. As the father of Mrs Mardon, I am desirous of stating a few particulars in relation thereto and also respectfully to solicit your patronage and support of Mrs Mardon for whose benefit I am desirous of continuing the business.
> It has long been painfully evident to myself as well as to most other persons that Mr Mardon's course of conduct was disreputable and ruinous, and I felt it my duty from regard to his wife and family to insist upon a speedy termination. After some consideration as to the best course to be adopted he agreed to sell me the business at a valuation, the proceeds to be divided among his creditors, and to give me the power of Attorney to act fully in his absence; the necessary documents were then prepared by Mr Wasbrough and duly executed.
> I have now become responsible for all goods supplied... and am desirous of being accepted as your tenant of the shop and premises as now occupied by Mrs Mardon, and trust that from her business habits as well as the kind expressions of sympathy and promises of support she has already received, that she will be enabled to carry on the business in all its branches with efficiency and success.
> Again earnestly soliciting your support,
> I am Gentlemen,
> Yours very respectfully
> George C Ashmead

The Committee decided to reduce the area occupied by Mrs Mardon and brick up the door communicating with the Club premises. A permanent manager would be installed above the 'Engine house' and given direct access to the Club via a doorway to be knocked through the party wall. Mr Hartland was then appointed at an annual salary of £100 and proceeded to manage the premises with great efficiency for the ensuing fifteen years.

Disregarding Mr Ashmead's pleas, the Committee served a Notice to Quit on Mrs Mardon within weeks. They were obviously dissatisfied with the arrangements regarding newspapers and periodicals and anxious to take over their supply. Defiantly, she chose to remain, however, and the uncomfortable situation was allowed to continue for another three years. As the breach widened, Mrs Mardon requested that all future communication should be in writing.

In 1860 half a dozen letters were exchanged between the Committee, who were eager to raise the annual rent, and Mr Ashmead, who was very much opposed to such an increase. The outcome was that the original rent was maintained for one year only — on the expiry of which Mrs Mardon agreed to move out. Much wrangling followed; the tenancy was prolonged at an increased rental, while the right to supply newspapers was twice withdrawn. Demanding and difficult to the last, Mrs Mardon left under a cloud when her rent cheque for the final quarter bounced.

National Provincial Bank

When Mrs Mardon finally relinquished the premises after a turbulent tenancy of five years, they were let to the National Provincial Bank at an annual rental of £180 on a seven-year lease. The opening of the bank was recorded on 22 January 1862 in the *Clifton Chronicle*, under the heading 'Bank for Clifton':

> We are happy to announce that a branch bank for Clifton, the desirability of which was suggested in these columns some time ago, was yesterday opened by the National Provincial Bank of England, temporarily, at the premises in occupation of Mrs Mardon, Mall Buildings.

The glazed partition, so useful for a bookseller who was also manager of the Club, was seen as a hazard for the bank — which would be separated from the Club premises by

The corner building on Caledonia Place, fronting The Mall, which is the present-day home of the National Westminster Bank. When the photograph was taken the premises were occupied by James Dryland's sports shop (see page 66)

means of the existing shutters, iron-lined and locked. The plate glass towards the corridor, however, was to be silvered and retained. To make the dividing wall uniform, the existing woodwork was continued across bricked-up doorways and a brick partition formed a connection with the back wall. After these initial alterations and some modernisation to the living quarters, costing £200 in all, the Club maintained good relations with the new tenant. Indeed, as a gesture of goodwill, the Committee decided to transfer its account from the Bank of the West of England to the bank on its own premises. This was also very convenient, as no other banks existed in Clifton at the time.

When the seventh year of the lease was nearing its conclusion, the bank manager inadvertently offended the Committee through a most indiscreet action. In the words of the Secretary:

> A printed circular which had been forwarded to the Manager by post, with reference to the establishment of a new club in Clifton, was placed before the Committee, from which it appeared that Mr Frederick Howard, the Manager of the Clifton Branch of the National Provincial Bank, the present bankers of this Association, had attached his name to such circular as one of the provisional committee for the formation of the new club. And the Committee considering that such a procedure was adverse to the interest of this Association, it was resolved that a special meeting of the Committee be summoned to take the conduct of Mr Howard into consideration and to decide whether any and what application should be made to the bank authorities on the subject.

The threat of a second club did not materialise, however, the Athenæum remaining the principal rival establishment in Bristol. In the event, and on reflection, the Committee resolved not to exact retribution.

In 1878 the corner building on Caledonia Place, immediately opposite, was adapted to house Bristol Old Bank — which was to become part of the National Provincial Bank forty years later, through various mergers. At first the two banks faced each other across the Mall, but in 1922 they eventually joined forces on the larger premises, where the National Westminster Bank still has a branch today.

Incidentally, the cellar excavated beneath the bookshop became a convenient strong room for the bank which succeeded the shop. It is still in use today, despite the unaccountable way in which a heavy metal door moves unaided and the mysterious tendency of certain objects to disappear!

12

The Tavern in Waterloo Street

Included in the premises purchased by the second Clifton Club was a functioning tavern, which seems to have occupied an area behind the Assembly Rooms on the ground and first floors. External access was from Waterloo Street (then known as Stable Lane), but there was also an internal door at first floor level, connecting the licensed premises with the main part of the building.

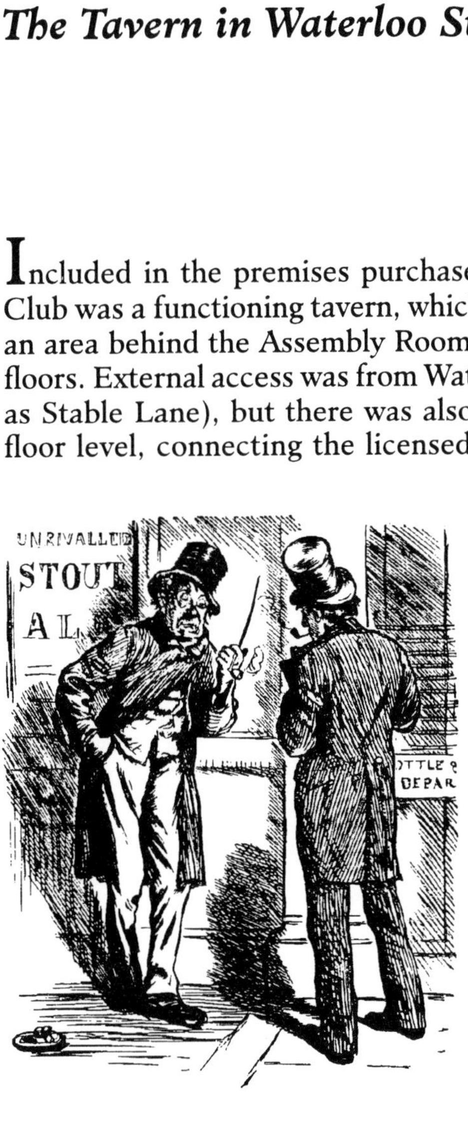

The tavern was usually referred to as the Shades or the Tap. In the original brief for the architect's conversion of the Royal Hotel, instructions regarding the rear of the premises were as follows: 'The Tap to be divided off from the rest of the Buildings, for a respectable Tavern'. However, only slight alterations were required here as — understandably — the Committee had second thoughts about dividing off such an appropriate establishment. It would seem that the premises at first floor level (usually known as the Shades) were to remain connected with the Club. The Tap, which was situated at street level, would have provided ale for local households, whose servants were sent with jugs to be filled.

The first landlord, Mr Pomeroy, proposed renting the Tap and adjoining living accommodation for the first five years at £70 per annum. He was duly summoned to a meeting of the Committee

> when it was represented to him that if he took the Tavern, the Committee could only let it for three years absolutely, without entering into any future arrangements as regarded the rent after that term — and that the floor on a level with the public rooms should be entirely appropriated to the use of the Subscribers.

Having been given time to reflect, Mr Pomeroy sent his reply the following day:

> Sir
> I have duly considered the proposition made at the meeting yesterday. I am come to the conclusion of having nothing more to do with the Royal Hotel Tap.
> I am Sir
> Yours obediently,
> W L Pomeroy

However, negotiations were resumed between solicitors, when it became clear that the rent required was £80 per annum. Ideally, the back entrance should be closed, so that the tavern might be part of the new Club and serve subscribers exclusively. Eventually Mr Pomeroy agreed to the conditions, managing the Shades and Tap for three years without any noteworthy misdemeanours. When the Committee decided to requisition the living quarters, he was unwilling to continue as landlord, but he remained a tenant in one of the Club's small dwellings in Waterloo Street.

The tenancy of the Tap and Wine Vaults was advertised in July 1860, when Mr Hooper was chosen to succeed Mr Pomeroy at a reduced rent of £50. His lease of the Tap included the Wine Vaults and the dwelling houses at 1 and 3 Waterloo Street. It appears that he sub-let No 3, which had reached an advanced state of disrepair by the time it was handed back to the Committee. When it had been put in order, he lived there himself.

The state of the tavern kitchen did not facilitate catering, but once this was rectified Mr Hooper supplied the members of the Club with food for a complete decade. In the end, it was the poor standard of his catering and the inferiority of wines supplied which brought about his downfall. After a warning, Mr Hooper was given his notice. He had succeeded in running the Tap and Refreshment Room longer than any other landlord, past or future, but this was apparently at the expense of quality.

Instead of advertising for a new tenant, the Committee decided to offer the vacancy to the original landlord, Mr Pomeroy, who was still living in rented accommodation in Waterloo Street. It was soon arranged that Mr Pomeroy should resume the tenancy of the Tap and the Wine Vaults, the rent being further reduced to £42 per annum — a reasonable indication that business was declining.

Meanwhile, the lease of Mr Hooper's rented house in Waterloo Street went to Mr Maggs, a builder, who proved at first to be a very satisfactory tenant, attending to many repairs and improvements himself. The Committee gave him a contribution of £2 and permission 'to fix a shaft on the upper part of the house rented by him in order to improve the light and ventilation in the back rooms'. They were also willing to foot the bill of £4.18.0d for a water closet to be installed in the house. Apparently an ideal tenant, Mr Maggs was soon granted a seven-year lease at £22 per annum. By 1874, however, he owed arrears of rent and was obliged to move out, Mr Otto Klemm succeeding him at £20 per annum.

Mr Pomeroy's second tenancy of the Tap and Wine Vaults lasted only one year, after which the position was advertised three times weekly in the Bristol papers until Mrs Isabella Butler (who had managed a hotel in Sherbourne) was appointed. A room was supplied by the Committee so that she could live on the premises at a rent of £30 per annum. A further £25 was to be charged for the Wine Vaults with their fixtures and part of the cellar. When a brick partition had been built, Mr Burgess (tenant of the Grocer's shop in The Mall) was to take the remaining area in the cellar for £10 annually on a fourteen-year lease.

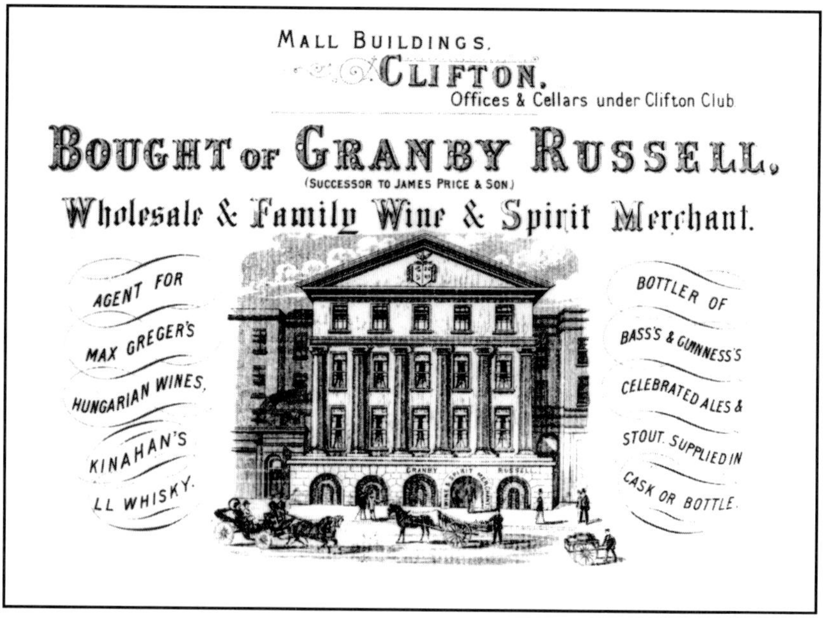

Advertisement from the 1870s promoting wine and spirits trade conducted from the Club cellars

The cellars had initially been let to Mr Henry Smith, who sold wine and bottled liquor from the premises, which he rented at £35 per annum. Mr Price then took over these premises for a period of fourteen years. After 1871, they seem to have been let to Granby Russell, partly in conjunction with the Tap. Interestingly, the original trade in wine and spirits has been perpetuated in different forms so that even today the same type of business is carried on in the cellars.

Mrs Butler had no success in running the tavern. After only a year she wrote to the Committee, stating that 'she was unable to pay the expenses of the waiter, that the receipts from the Club and business of the Shades were not sufficient to enable her to pay her way'. She withdrew in 1872 to be replaced by Mr Thomas Brown, then living at 3 Boyce's Buildings, 'a person well known in Clifton and calculated to improve the business'. The tenacious Mr Brown managed the Shades for a full two years before standing down.

His successor, Mr Otto Klemm, soon ran into trouble with the police — on the grounds that he was supplying alcohol to members of the Club after hours, via the internal connecting door. One day in early September 1875,

> Superintendent Thatcher handed notice to Mr Dawes, the Manager, intimating proceedings against Mr Otto Klemm for having internal communication with rooms of the Club. Dr Marshall explained (to the Committee) that the licence extended through the whole of the Rooms and that, while the licence existed, the Rooms must be closed at 11 o'clock.

Although this was a state of affairs which had tacitly existed for nineteen years under all the previous landlords, the Committee was now in an embarrassing situation and needed a scapegoat. It was considered expedient 'to give Mr Otto Klemm notice to quit on the 25th March 1876'. All internal communication between the Club premises and the Shades was immediately suspended, the door being bricked up without delay.

It was also decided that the Secretary 'should communicate at once with the licensing authorities... with a

view to prevent any renewal of the licence extending to any part of the Club'. He later reported to the Committee that

> he had arranged with Mr Klemm the terms of the Royal Hotel Shades respecting the licence granted by the Excise for his house for the sale of spirituous liquors etc and that licences now comprised only the Royal Hotel Shades as occupied by him and did not extend to any part of the Club Rooms.

As might be expected, the separation of the Club from the tavern was an unpopular move, particularly with Mr Klemm, whose receipts dropped to such an extent that he applied to the Committee for compensation. With rent hopelessly in arrears, he moved away from Clifton after handing over to landlord number six, Mr Tibbatts. As both house and tavern were in a bad state of repair, it was necessary to expend £20.15.0d on renovations before the new tenant would consent to sign the agreement. Only six months later, the Committee was surprised to hear that Mr Tibbatts was ready to move on 'in consequence of the illness of his wife'.

The seventh landlord of the Shades, Mr Powell of Stourbridge had only been in residence four months when he changed his mind. He was succeeded by Mr John Williams, formerly landlord of the Suspension Bridge Inn.

And the eighth landlord, Mr Williams, had been running the tavern for approximately seven months when he decided that, with the Committee's blessing, Mr Tassaker would make a good successor.

When severed from most of its clientele (club members, who were served via the connecting door) the tavern was no longer a viable business since there was little passing trade in Waterloo Street. To make matters worse, Clifton seemed to have lost its air of prosperity. Could it be that the popularity of the area was waning? According to a comment at the AGM held in March 1875, the keepers of Clifton lodging houses and hotels were suffering from a marked lack of custom in the 1870s,

owing to the smaller number of visitors and temporary residents there had been in the place, on account of reports that unhealthiness prevailed in the district, caused by sewer gas etc.

Potential customers may even have been influenced by 'the smell arising from Mr Smith's Fish Shop', which merited a letter of complaint from the Sanitary Inspector.

With the ninth landlord, Mr Tassaker, who was presumably the last, both Tap and Shades quietly disappear from the records.

13

Administrative Problems

Financial questions frequently dominated the meetings of the Committee which was responsible for running the second Clifton Club from its opening in 1856. As could have been anticipated, the cost of providing suitable accommodation for the new club had considerably exceeded the original estimate. This meant that the project was launched on a deficit, a state of affairs which caused anxiety among the proprietors for many years. At the second Annual General Meeting of the Assocciation, held in March 1858, it was reported that:

> The capital of the Society consists of £10,000. £6,000 of this sum has been raised by the creation of 120 shares of £50 each and the remaining £4,000 on a mortgage of the premises. The total expenditure is £10,936 of which the following is an analysis:

Original contracts for the alteration of premises	*£3,194. 7. 8*
Purchase money including the costs of conveyance	*4,311. 8. 0*
Extra works including decorating, papering etc	*1,152.10.11*
Furnishing including billiard tables, chandeliers, fixtures	*1,250. 3. 0*
Architect and Clerk of the Works	*555. 0. 0*
Preliminary expenses	*251.18. 5*
Interest on paid-up capital	*221. 0. 3*
	£10,936. 8. 3

This leaves a deficiency. Your Committee are inclined to recommend that the proprietors raise it among themselves by the creation of 120 £10 shares to be divided amongst the shareholders according to the number of shares held by them, in effect increasing each share to £60.

Shareholders expected to receive dividends, usually 5% gross, but this reduced the annual reserve by 75% and eventually began to irritate members. It was found that any surplus which could have been used for maintenance or improvements was largely being paid out as 'pettifogging dividends'. To compound this, another potential source of income was being neglected. Comparable London clubs were levying an entrance fee of forty guineas, but there was no entrance fee for the club established in the former Assembly Rooms and the Committee persisted in their refusal to introduce one. Such financial disagreements caused tension between proprietors and members for some twenty-five years until a very radical change in the constitution was proposed at a meeting held in 1880:

Having regard to the conflicting interests of the Proprietors of the Clifton Subscriptions Rooms Association on the one hand and the subscribers to the Club on the other hand, with regard to the amount of expense annually incurred for the maintenance

> and management of the Club, it is desirable to consider whether it may not be for the advantage of both parties that the affairs of the Club should no longer be managed by the Committee of the Association and that the Committee be requested to consider the practicability of letting the Club furnished to such person or persons as may be willing to take a lease of the same for the purposes of a Club and to report to the Proprietors on what terms such a lease should be granted.

At a subsequent meeting, it was resolved that it would be desirable to let the Subscription Rooms furnished to tenants approved by the Committee at an annual rent of £300. While there was general agreement on this matter, nothing was actually done about it until 1882, when something more urgent — the question of Sunday opening — forced the issue.

Comparison with other clubs had produced the realisation that many of these opened their doors on a Sunday whereas the Clifton Club remained steadfastly closed. The members were understandably very fond of their premises, a second home where they could escape from their womenfolk and worldly pressures. However, they were regularly denied access to this haven every Sunday. Among non-clerical members there was an increasing dissatisfaction at the six-day rule, which assumed that gentlemen had more important things to do on Sunday, when the doors of the Club remained locked. The membership also included a number of clergy, who were adamant that Sunday was a day on which to abstain from pleasurable things and suppressed the fact that the Reading Room of the original Club had in fact been opened for four hours each Sunday afternoon. It was obviously impossible to please both factions.

This Victorian dilemma was broached at the eighteenth AGM in 1874, when the Chairman explained that opening the Club on Sunday would not be consistent with the deed of settlement. At the nineteenth AGM, a member pointed out that most clubs in England and abroad were open on Sunday, and suggested that religious and theological works might be placed on the tables to promote a suitable frame of mind. Or prayers could be said in the Reading Room. (This seemed to amuse the meeting.) The Secretary commented that when the

Club was established, the large ecclesiastical element among the shareholders had ensured that the deed of settlement was drawn up 'with a view to render it practically impossible to open the rooms on Sunday'. The only way round this would be to wind up the Association and reconstitute it under a new deed.

It was agreed that a circular should be prepared and addressed to each shareholder or trustee asking whether they would consent to the rooms being opened on Sunday or, if not, on what terms they would part with their shares. One member caused a great deal of merriment on stating his fear that 'if the inducement of a high price for their shares were held out to objecting proprietors, a very large number would be seized with conscientious scruples on the Sunday question!'

The following circular was accordingly prepared and sent out in July 1875:

> Sir,
> I am requested by the Committee to inform you that at the Annual General Meeting of this Association held on the 1st of March instant, a resolution was unanimously passed to the effect that a circular should be addressed to every proprietor to ascertain his opinion as to the advisability of opening the Subscription Rooms on Sundays, to meet the wishes of a large number of subscribing members. In accordance with the resolution, I now beg to enquire if you approve of or object to the proposed alteration, and I shall feel obliged by your filling up the enclosed form of Assent or Dissent, and by your forwarding the same to me at your very earliest convenience.
> I am, Dear Sir,
> Yours Very Truly
> Ambrose E Nash (Honorary Secretary)

Although 51 members were in agreement (approximately half), 39 failed to reply and 11 were decidedly against the proposal. In the circumstances no further action could be taken.

There was a large attendance at the twentieth AGM, 1876, as it was known in advance that this controversial issue would again be raised. The local newspaper reported:

> Mr C B Hare brought forward the subject of having the Club opened on Sundays. He alluded to the desirability to the members of having the dining, smoking and reading rooms open on a Sunday, and said there were at least 70 shareholders who had signified their assent to such an arrangement. A lengthy discussion ensued on the subject, and ultimately it was resolved 'that the Committee be directed to take measures for opening the Club on Sundays or for reconstituting the Society so as to enable the proprietors to do so'. The members were for the most part desirous of having an alteration and though a few at the meeting were opposed to the innovation, no-one spoke against the proposal.

At the next meeting of the Committee Mr Burroughs, who had presided over the AGM as Chairman, vacated the chair by way of protest. As the proposal at the AGM had been passed unanimously, it was then resolved that the back reading room, smoking room and dining room should be open from 2.00 to 8.00pm on Sundays, while the card and billiard rooms should not be opened on any account.

To mark their strong objection, the Chairman and another prominent member resigned their seats on the Committee. Two gentlemen were designated to visit and try to induce them to withdraw their resignations, but in vain. His principles uncompromised, Mr Burroughs remained adamant:

> Feeling it to be impossible to become a party to the proposed violation of the stipulations in the deed of settlement... I must adhere to the determination expressed in my letter of withdrawing altogether from the Committee.

Meanwhile, an indignant letter of protest was received, signed by five other members (including the Rev Wallace and the Rev Rickards) who demanded that the resolution be rescinded. When this letter failed to produce any result, the outraged members engaged a solicitor to express their views at length:

> We cannot suppose that the Committee will, in defiance of the Deed under which they derive their powers as managers of the Rooms, continue in a course which, whatever may be the wishes of the majority of the shareholders, cannot but be illegal, and we therefore imagine that it can only be necessary as an evidence of determination on the part of those gentlemen we represent, for us to say that should the Rooms be opened again on Sunday, we have instructions from some of those gentlemen to apply at once for an injunction to restrain any further breach of the provisions of the Trust Deed.

After discussion of the solicitor's threatened action, the chastened Committee decided not to implement the Sunday opening resolution made just one month previously at the twentieth AGM. An apologetic notice was pinned up in the Club:

The Committee regret to inform the Members that they deem it prudent to close the Club on Sundays for the present.

Totally alienated from the Clifton Club by this time, two of the objecting members sold their shares, while the Chairman refused to be reinstated. After such a fiasco, the Sunday-opening faction lay low for five years prior to approaching the problem from a more legal angle. Solicitors were then instructed to obtain the opinion of Counsel with a view to applying to the Court of Chancery for certain offending clauses to be expunged from the Deed.

In January 1882, on receiving the legal advice requested, the Committee resolved 'that steps be taken forthwith for the dissolution of the Association and for the formation of a new Company in accordance with the advice of Counsel'. An Extraordinary General Meeting was called on 16 February 1882 to consider the following proposals:

1. That it is expedient that the Association should be dissolved.

2. That the Trustees be at liberty, upon the dissolution of the Association, to sell all the undertaking and property of the Association, (subject to its debts and liabilities) to the Clifton Club Company Ltd, in consideration of the net sum of £9,000 to be paid by the said company in cash, or in such number of fully paid-up shares in the said company as the respective Shareholders in the Association, entitled to share in the division of such purchase moneys, may be willing to accept in lieu of cash, with the balance in cash.

It is proposed that the Capital of the new Company shall be £12,000 divided into 160 shares of £75 each, and that every Shareholder in the present Association shall be entitled, in lieu of each share of £60 now held by him, to a fully paid-up share to the value of £75 (plus 5% dividend as previously).

These resolutions were carried unanimously. It had taken seven years to override the objections of the clergy and moralists, and this time there were no legal loopholes. The Club had to become a tenant on its own premises in order to obtain access to them seven days a week.

14

Handover to the Clifton Club Company

Generally speaking, members were greatly relieved to be renting their own premises at £300 annually, and satisfied with the total purchase price of £9,000. But they had not forgotten their underlying grievances with regard to the previous running of the Club. Some of these were aired at the last AGM of the old regime on 6 March 1882, which was also the first to be held under the auspices of the Clifton Club Company.

> Dr Marshall brought forward a proposal to authorise the expenditure of £1,200 in alterations and improvements on the club premises, and hoped the governing body of the new company would be influenced in the direction of improvements; for so far from there being any improvement in the character of the club since it was established twenty-five years ago, it had rather deteriorated and they now missed accommodations which they then possessed... He attributed the decline which they had to deplore to shares in the Association being more largely taken up as an investment than at first was the case; the original shareholders having taken part in the project primarily with a view to benefitting Clifton and making it socially more attractive by the establishment of a good club, and not for the purpose of making a profit. When the investment element, however, got the upper hand, comfort and convenience were postponed to pettifogging dividend, to such an extent that they could not even afford a hall porter, a deficiency in which they were, as a club, almost unique, and visitors had to find their way as best they could.

The Clifton Club Company created a lot of goodwill among members by acting on this proposal. By the winter, major improvements had been carried out and in January 1883 a memorable ball was held on the premises to celebrate their completion. It was clear that standards were rising when it was announced that a hall porter's lad (at five shillings a week) and another charwoman were to be employed, while the lighting of a fire in the upstairs Smoking Room on Sundays would increase the comfort of the members.

As soon as the Clifton Club Company took over, a book was purchased for suggestions or complaints, which would make interesting reading later on. Another refinement was the provision of a book 'in which members will be at liberty to insert notices or advertisements on any subject in which they may be personally interested (such for instance as a description of any horse or carriage which they may have for sale or may wish to purchase)'. Sparing no cost, the Clifton Club Company then updated the works of reference in the Reading Room.

A second dial (to cost no more than £6) was ordered from the local clockmaker, Mr Cordeux, so that the Reading Room clock could simultaneously show the time in the Billiard Room. This meant that the pendulum and weights hung in a cavity inside the wall between these rooms. When the bricked-up recess below the clock was re-opened in 1992, over a century later, the pendulum and weights were removed to make room for glazed doors, but the two-faced timepiece, now electrically operated, remains functional.

It is worth mentioning that in 1884 this more relaxed financial situation facilitated the installation of the telephone. In 1886, only four years after the initial improvements had been carried out, a generous sum of £700 was allocated for a comprehensive programme of redecoration involving every detail of the interior of the Club premises.

Entrance Hall and Staircases
Thoroughly cleaned and repainted in three coats.
Hinges of old doors removed.
Skirting of cement and dado rail fixed to staircases.
Clock from Billiard Room fixed over door of Lavatory.

Large Reading Room
Repainted and decorated. Old decorations removed.
Walls painted in three coats. Columns painted and gilt.
Gilt beadings round all arches.
Entablature under clock removed and clock face decorated to match and another face placed in Billiard Room.
Handsome cornice and frieze.
Partition opposite clock removed and new arched ceiling placed in vestibule.
Vestibule much improved.
One new gas bracket and four old rebronzed and divers new door handles.
Curtain fixed in arch of vestibule. New plate glass fixed in entrance door.
Door fitted with patent closer. Four doors painted and decorated.
Cement skirting placed round room. Four niches cut down to level of floor.
Floor: Inequalities removed. Patent Victoria Axminster carpet laid down.

Margins stained and varnished, felt placed under carpet.
Fireplaces: Mantelpieces and mirrors repainted.
Old stone fenders removed and brass fenders substituted.
Hearths laid with encaustic tiles.
Ventilation: Altered and improved.
Furniture: Centre table and twelve chairs repaired and covered in best Morocco leather. Four writing tables also so treated.
Four chairs provided for writing tables and four electric bells fitted.
Two old settees altered and covered with Morocco leather and placed in two of the recesses.

Large Billiard Room
Walls and ceiling painted in two coats. Paper cornice.
Six settees altered and improved and covered with Morocco.
New floor cloth laid down. Cue racks and doors covered with cloth.
Marble mantelpieces repaired. Six gas brackets fixed.
Notice board provided. Ventilation altered. New clock face introduced.

Small Billiard Room
Ceiling and walls thoroughly cleaned and recoloured.
Another ventilator placed in flue.
Lobby at Head of Staircase.
Painted in four coats.
Dado rail provided also in Telephone Lobby.

Passage to Committee Room
Old partitions removed, thoroughly cleaned, papered and painted.
New urinal provided. Cover placed in sink. Gas pipes and brackets altered.

Staircase to Smoking Room
Cleaned and painted in two coats. Dado rail fixed.

Members were delighted with the comfort and convenience achieved since the change of management. Further structural alterations, costing £2,000, were completed in 1890, and some new furniture and fittings were ordered; the total cost of £1,141 was to be 'liquidated gradually'. As a result, certain policy changes regarding expenditure became noticeable, which helped to reduce the

A 1950s photograph showing the alterations carried out to the first-floor windows of the Club building in 1893

adverse balance to £913 by the end of 1892. The following year, as an additional economy measure, members were asked to contribute to a Furniture Fund for the Front Reading Room, which was to be converted to a Smoking Room. At the same time, the Clifton Club Company was requested to carry out expensive and unnecessary alterations to the windows in that room — alterations which would completely change the appearance of the facade. The existing windows were to be replaced by three plain and two bay windows, reluctantly designed by Mr Edwards, the new consultant architect. This explains the rather incongruous line of windows in alternating style at first floor level today.

The general refurbishment was financed by members through their Furniture Fund, which had raised £250. A total of £38 was to be spent on the redecoration of the Front Room. An Axminster carpet, at £46.10.0d, was ordered from Hancock's, together with new curtains, blinds and curtain poles (£26.3.0d in all). A number of chairs were recovered in Morocco and renovated, while the only new items of furniture were a bookcase and a smoking table, upon which the brass cigar lighter presented by Mr Benson of Broad Street must have looked very elegant. The installation of electrical lighting circuits in certain rooms, which had cost the Clifton Club Company £50, now involved selecting shades for the various electroliers.

The regular annual expenses included two guineas towards watering the roads, two guineas for the upkeep of the Mall Gardens, one guinea to the beadle of the district etc. Such commitments had to be respected. However, the Committee dispensed with the services of Mr Cordeux, whose annual fee for winding up and regulating the clocks which he had originally provided was two guineas. Further economy measures, such as the closure of rooms and dismissal of staff, failed to put the Club on an even keel financially. An explanatory letter was addressed to each member, suggesting an increase in subscriptions.

> Dear Sir
> The subject of the finances of the Club has for some time past anxiously engaged the attention of your Committee, and they desire to lay a statement before you prior to the General Meeting to be held on April 30th 1896. The total indebtedness of the Club now amounts to £1,115.6.9d. Having carefully considered the matter, and making allowance for every possible economy, your Committee do not see their way to confine the annual expenses within the limits of the present revenue, if the Club is to be kept up on the same lines.
> It must be remembered that of recent years the Club premises have been largely extended; new rooms have not only been

added but old ones brought into use; and the facilities and advantages to Members greatly increased. These improvements, step by step, have been sanctioned by General Meetings, but no provision has ever been made for the additional expenses which such extensions necessarily involved. It was no doubt hoped that the advantages which the Club can now offer — scarcely second to any in the provinces — would attract additional members. This reasonable expectation has not hitherto been fulfilled.

The Committee wish to point out that the income derived from entrance fees and subscriptions is not sufficient to meet the expenses of the ordinary working and maintenance of the Club. The separate accounts of Dining Room, Billiard Room and Card Room all show substantial profits; without this the adverse balance of the year would be largely increased.

Your Committee therefore are desirous of enquiring if, under the present emergency, you would be willing that the annual subscription of members should be increased by One Guinea until the number of members in the Club and the increase of its revenue shall warrant the Committee in discontinuing such addition.

Despite the favourable response of a large majority, there was a change of heart at the fourteenth AGM , held on 30 April 1896:

The Committee felt that great deference was due to the opinion of the minority. They therefore with regret but unanimously abandoned all idea of proposing an increased subscription, and the only course that remained open to them was to frame an estimate on the lines of the most rigid economy curtailing many of the advantages most valued by many members of the Club.

Servants who left the Club were not replaced, the telegram service was to be discontinued. Possibly depressed by the situation, one member of the Committee, Mr W Fairbanks, resigned his membership on the grounds of a nervous breakdown, for which he had been 'imperatively ordered by a first-rate London doctor to take a long voyage at once'.

Towards the end of 1896, another way of increasing revenue was adopted: the entrance fee of five guineas was waived for a few weeks to encourage applications from new members. With over fifty names proposed, this ploy proved to be a great success. To increase the range of gentlemen eligible for membership, the rules were changed in March 1897 to include country members who might fall into one of the following categories:

(a) Those who reside outside a radius of seven miles from the Club and have no office or place of business within that radius

(b) Undergraduates at any of the universities

(c) Cadets at Sandhurst or Woolwich

This would not alter the general character of the Club, as such members would only be admitted for a maximum of twenty days a year.

Thanks to these measures, the number of members had risen by one third in the spring of 1898 to a record total exceeding four hundred. The revenue thereby generated decreased the adverse balance to £843.10.2d from £1,000 the previous year, despite certain domestic expenses.

By 1898, the building was still partially gas-lit. The Reading Room was next on the list for conversion by the Club Company, and the Committee could see their way to spending approximately £23 on six 'electric light standards' which would illuminate the writing tables. This may have been prompted by past accidents with the oil lamps which were used in conjunction with gas brackets in the Reading Room. One had recently burst, for instance, causing damage to a writing table, the repair of which (amounting to £1.4.6d) had been charged to the Law Union & Crown Fire Insurance Company. Indicative of improved finances, a specially designed plate glass screen was subsequently commissioned for the Reading Room (probably as protection from the ubiquitous draughts) and two Turkey carpets were ordered.

More architectural alterations were suggested in the final year of the century. By this time there was a Streets Improvement Committee, which approved the plans for a new entrance porch to the building. However, as it would encroach on the pavement, building permission was granted on the proviso that the Club Company paid five shillings annually and agreed to demolish the porch if necessary. In the circumstances, the Club finally decided against further altering the façade.

The early years of the twentieth century saw the installation of electric lighting in the Card Room and the extension of electrical circuits in other parts of the building. The Clifton Club Company contributed half the cost although at the time it was involved with the repair and repainting of the back of the premises in Waterloo Street.

The adverse balance had sunk to £479.9.1d by the AGM of 1900, but this debt meant that all proposed expenditure was pared down to a minimum. In fact the Estimate of Income and Expenditure for 1907 was rejected as likely to greatly increase the deficit. Drastic changes were required. A sub-committee appointed to consider the position made the following suggestions:

(a) That the Club Company be requested to reduce the rent for a period of two years.

(b) That the necessary steps be taken to obtain a reduction of the assessment of the Club premises for rates.

(c) That in place of the existing system, a contract should be made for twelve months' coal supply.

(d) That the Secretary's offer to take a reduced salary of

£150 per annum be accepted.

(e) That a reduction of at least £20 per annum be made in the amount paid for periodicals and newspapers.

(f) That telegrams be discontinued at a saving of at least £20 per annum.

(g) That the tender of Foster's Laundry Company for washing, at a reduction of roughly 33%, should be accepted — a saving of about £8.

(h) That expenditure on postages is excessive.

(i) That a saving of £3 or £4 should be made in connection with the Library Subscription.

As bait to lure new members, it was also recommended that the entrance fee should be waived for the first half of 1907 and reinstated at only two guineas for the rest of that year.

The Clifton Club Company responded handsomely, donating £100 to the Club. With financial pressures temporarily alleviated, additional lighting circuits were again considered, starting with the Dining Room. Electrical fittings, shades and metal filament lamps (at nearly five shillings each) further increased the outlay. The billiard table in the Lower Room received electrical illumination next, followed by the Back Reading Room. Having used various private firms in the past, the Club was now engaging the electrical department of the Corporation of Bristol to estimate and carry out the work. Their estimate for wiring the Upper Billiard Room for instance, was £12.6.3d including fittings.

By 1912 more expensive items were pending, such as the necessary replacement of the Turkey stair carpet, the total cost of which would be £30.7.10d. However careful the Committee was, there were always new items and areas that needed updating or refurbishment. And it proved impossible to minimise the deficit without neglecting the material condition of the premises. As a last resort, a deficiency fund was opened and members were appealed to for contributions. Some headway was made, mainly due to a donation of £200 from the Clifton Club Company, but the adverse balance persisted through the First World War, before being finally dealt with in a quite unexpected way.

The constitution set up in 1882 survived for more than a century, until 1996, when a new company was formed to protect the future of the Club by a restructuring of the shareholding.

15

Nineteenth Century Communications

Electric Telegraph

In addition to its use for lighting and bell systems, electricity facilitated long-distance communication. The electric telegraph system was launched a quarter of a century before the telephone and run as a monopoly by the Post Office. This was a great improvement on the preceding shutter and semaphore systems, which were only used on a few fixed routes to manually transmit coded news from certain ports to the Admiralty in London — or, functioning in reverse, to issue instructions. Both these visual systems of long-distance communication, reminiscent of the lines of hilltop beacons in use in many civilisations from earliest times, were invented by ingenious Frenchmen during the Napoleonic Wars. The network which they established helped to unite Napoleon's new empire by the rapid transmission of news. Ironically, when the British copied the invention, it was to avoid becoming part of the French Empire by sending early warning of potential invasion from the south coast to London. These visual telegraph systems, which were adopted by many countries during the first half of the nineteenth century, were cumbersome to run and limited to good visibility in the hours of daylight. The advent of electricity quickly rendered them obsolete.

From 1850 onwards, news could be instantaneously

transmitted by the electric telegraph without being relayed between intermediate stations, subject to light and weather conditions. In times of international unrest or warfare the only means of obtaining fresh news from the scene of action was to subscribe to the Post Office, which would then provide hand-written telegrams for public display on a special stand. These abbreviated versions of the latest news, corresponding to our news bulletins, were considerably more up-to-date than accounts in the newspapers — which eventually arrived by train from London. Appropriate signals were transmitted along electrical wires which followed the course of the recently constructed railway lines radiating from London to major cities. On receipt at provincial post offices, each message was copied and relayed to subscribers as a hand-written telegram.

At the Clifton Club a telegram stand, which was among the original furnishing items, seems to have been in use almost as soon as the Club opened its doors in 1856. Although there was considerable resistance to the expense involved in subscribing to the system, the Committee indulged in the luxury of fresh news whenever England was

engaged in warfare. The telegram stand would be centrally placed for the benefit of members, who gathered to read the succession of telegraphic despatches as they arrived. When the Telegraphic Company increased its annual subscription to £40 in 1859 the Committee decided to dispense with telegrams. However, it was probably due to the advent of the telephone that prices later sank to 1d per message 'written in text hand', and the service was accordingly reinstated in 1887. During the Boer War which commenced in 1899, Central News Ltd supplied war telegrams between 8am and midnight at a monthly rate of £4.17.0d. The Post Office Telegraph Company, responsible for all transmission, was permitted to attach a single wire to the large chimney stack on the roof of the Club in exchange for a nominal rental of one shilling a year.

There seemed to be one major drawback with this modern technology: the handwriting was often illegible, in spite of repeated complaints to the local post office. As a last resort, the following letter was addressed to the Postmaster General:

> Dear Sir
> The Committee of the Clifton Club desire me to write and ask if you will kindly instruct the officials at the Clifton Post Office to be much more careful in the writing of telegrams we have sent to us. I enclose a specimen which I think you will admit is so faint that it is almost illegible. We have made several complaints to the local office, but they have had no effect whatever. So we should be much obliged if you would see that the writing in future is very much better and more distinct. The lines are too close together and the letters are badly formed. I should also be obliged if you could kindly suggest any other method by which the telegrams could be sent us in a more legible way as at present complaints by our members are frequent.
> Yours obediently,
> Herbert Nash, Honorary Secretary.

Telephone

When the Clifton Club was opened in the Mall, members would use the embossed notepaper for their letters, dropping them into the official letter box installed by the Post Office in the lobby, or persuading one of the servants to deliver a message by hand. Until the 1870s these were the

only ways of communicating with the outside world.

Always in the vanguard where new inventions were concerned, the Clifton Club Committee was interested in the possibility of transmitting speech by electricity — a concept which reached London in 1876 when Alexander Graham Bell was granted his patent. Three years later, when the first telephone exchange in the West Country was opened in the High Street, Bristol, the novelty was brought nearer home. In those early days, however, the Exchange had only twenty-five subscribers, all businessmen, who paid the elevated rental of £20 annually for an unmetered service during office hours, six days a week. Initially the radius covered was only one mile, which meant that Clifton lay outside the area served.

By 1881 the number of Bristol subscribers had quadrupled, and a subsidiary exchange was opened in Oakfield Grove, Clifton, to serve the private houses of city businessmen, using the Clifton prefix 55/56. At last the prospect of joining the élite on the telephone network had become a reality. In 1884 negotiations with the United Telephone Company were commenced 'for attaching the telephone to the club at a cost not exceeding £15 per annum'. The following deal was arranged:

> Mr Lewis, Manager of the telephone company, was willing to let the club have the use of the telephone for three months free of charge if the Committee grant him way leave for twelve months for a post on the roof of the club to be fixed... the same to be removed on giving six months' notice at any time. After the lapse of the above term of three months, the rent of the telephone to be £15 per annum if it suits the Company and this Committee

to allow it to remain.

A telephone was accordingly installed in the 'telephone lobby', where it soon became indispensable. Surprisingly, the annual rental was reduced even further to only £9 when a seven-year agreement was signed in 1891. Meanwhile, the telephone pole remained on the roof of the Club, ensuring low charges. It even indicated which way the wind was blowing — after a weathercock had been attached to it at the request of an eccentric doctor residing in Rodney Place!

At that time, the city skyline was becoming progressively more enmeshed with wires since all subscribers' circuits ran across housetops, doubtless supported by similar posts. They met at the main exchange in the High Street, as described in the *Bristol Observer*, October 1894:

> A great array of wires converge at the derrick upon the roof and their insulations form a huge bundle which goes down into the uppermost room of the Exchange where, in a long frame, they are sorted out, each being carried to its proper number... The wires descend to the switchroom... Young ladies sitting in front of the multiple switchboards have each to attend to the calls of 66 subscribers. Under the recently introduced system, the subscriber turns the handle of the instrument in his office and the electro-magnetic machine thus moved sends a current to the switch room. It causes a tiny electro-magnet to attract to itself a little lever, and... releases a flap right in front of the operator responsible... After the signal flap falls, she connects her telephone with the subscriber's wire by a simple spring adjustment; she hears from him the number, calls

> that subscriber by ringing his bell, and joins the caller and the called with a flexible conductor... 500 messages a day pass over the trunk lines in Bristol, while there are 11,500 local calls.

Access to telephones was gradually being extended to the public as 'call rooms' were opened. When the telephone at the Club was in use it was possible to use the call room at the bookseller's shop in the Mall, opened in 1886, or walk to the Clifton Exchange. The cost for three minutes' conversation was two pence. The popularity of these telephone centres increased to such an extent that there were twenty-five in Bristol and Clifton by 1895.

It would seem that Clifton Club members were not expected to pay for their calls until 1912, when a penny-in-the-slot box was fixed to the telephone in consequence of the increased rental demanded by the Post Office, which finally took over from the private telephone companies.

For short-distance communication, the speaking tube (at £1) was an inexpensive solution. Three years after the telephone was installed, the Committee arranged for such a tube to connect the club premises with an adjoining house let to an employee.

Towards the end of the century, the National Telephone Company applied to the Club for access to the pole on the roof raised by its predecessor, the United Telephone Company, and surmounted by a weathercock. As a result, they were permitted 'to place a small pipe up the wall at the back of the Club to convey a small cable for the purpose of connecting the wires upon the standard with an underground system', the telephone rental being reduced by £2 annually by way of compensation. This was an initial step towards burying the cat's cradle of rooftop wires which converged so unaesthetically upon the Telephone Exchange. Although the underground distribution has largely been achieved, various buildings are still festooned with telephone and other wires, even today.

16

Getting About

Early members of the Clifton Club were local residents, who considered that a brisk walk to the Mall — in clement weather — was healthy exercise. Any hopes that this might be combined with walking the household dog were soon dashed by Rule 20: 'No member is on any account to bring a dog into the Rooms'. Ways were found of side-stepping this rule, however, and dogs were admitted to the premises without actually being seen in the Rooms. After thirty years of such misinterpretation, the Committee of the second Clifton Club recommended altering the rule 'so as to exclude dogs altogether from the precincts of the Club and not from the Rooms only'.

When the weather was inclement — or in the case of members living further afield — a horse-drawn carriage was used. These private conveyances were kept in the many mews buildings at the rear of more imposing residences, while the liveried coachmen held a superior rank in the hierarchy of

domestic staff. Horses or carriages for sale could be advertised in a book kept at the Club for the benefit of members. In addition to private transport, a rank of hansom cabs for hire was conveniently situated on the Mall to facilitate the members' homeward journey, which often took place in the small hours after an enjoyable evening filled with cigar smoke and whisky-enhanced anecdotes.

In the early nineteenth century any journey by road could result in unexpected adventures, often as a consequence of the appalling condition of road surfaces. The old road between Bristol and Clifton was no exception, but new links constructed between the Clifton terraces were planned by the Merchant Venturers and had the additional advantage of technical advice from McAdam himself — also known as the 'Colossus of Roads'. By a coincidence, McAdam settled in Bristol soon after 1800, living in a series of houses in Park Street and Berkeley Square (as a plaque outside No 23 recalls).

The Bristol Trust was the first to realise the value of McAdam's road-making techniques, benefitting the city by appointing him General Surveyor in 1816. During his eight years in office, he transformed the 146 miles of local roads which had been 'all but impassable in bad weather'. His method was to raise the general level of roads while reducing the camber and insisting on the use of small broken stones, closely packed to a depth of ten inches. Rigid foundations and water-absorbent infill were omitted. McAdam described other measures taken in the Bristol area (which incidentally provided employment for the poor as well):

> I lowered a great number of hills, lengthened twenty bridges and widened the whole of the road between Bristol and Bath. Other lines of roads were widened and I also took down Black Horse Hill... Moreover we have made twelve miles of new roads... There has been a saving of £3,000 a year on the repair and upkeep of the roads since I took them over.

As a result, admiring Trusts up and down the country, sought his free advice and help in subsequent years. On the basis of his Bristol model, McAdam improved the national road network to a point where many hundreds of mail coaches were traversing the country daily without mishap. In fact he was responsible for the successful coaching era which facilitated the industrial revolution and preceded the building of railways. After all, 'roads may be called the veins and arteries of a country, through which channels every improvement circulates'.

Velocipedes

When the Mall premises were purchased in 1856, people were dependent on horse-power for most distances covered by road, as had been the case for countless centuries. But experiments were soon to result in rider-propelled machines that would make the horse virtually redundant. In 1869 a structure of wood and iron consisting basically of two equal wheels and pedals was demonstrated in London to incredulous

onlookers who had been convinced that it was impossible to remain upright on such a contraption. The device had been imported from Paris, where a mania for circulating on velocipedes had seized the upper classes. The novelty appealed to affluent young gentlemen, and the new boneshakers, as they were known, were manufactured in England to satisfy what seemed to be a transient fashion. The flat iron tyres of the French device were replaced by solid rubber, the size of the front wheel grew disproportionately and a rear step was fitted for dismounting purposes.

The respectable members of the Clifton Club would certainly have heard of the boneshaker, as it was reproduced and commented upon in the illustrated papers. The Spectator, for example, to which the Club subscribed, printed a very positive article:

> Bicycle riding, like skating, combines the pleasure of personal display with the luxury of swift motion through the air. The pursuit admits too of ostentation, as the machine can be adorned with almost any degree of visible luxury; and differences of price and, so to speak, of caste in the vehicle, can be made as apparent as in a carriage.

The disadvantages were also mentioned:

> The labour of forcing it along any rough road is calculated to be nearly equal to that of walking, but up an incline it is infinitely greater — greater in fact than if the traveller had to carry the velocipede.

Then there were problems with the heavy front wheel, which tended to change direction with every thrust of the pedals and needed continual adjustment via the handlebars.

There is no record of any Club member changing his means of transport from a carriage to one of the early velocipedes. And the increased size of the front wheel — culminating in the penny-farthing — would have severely restricted the number of potential riders. High-wheelers, introduced in 1870, were associated with danger and this was willingly accepted by addicts, who tended to be young, wealthy and agile. Any obstacle encountered on the

'The Clifton Assembly Rooms', painted by Rolinda Sharples, depicts a scene in the central room of the building, which is better known today as the Reading Room

A comfortable corner for correspondence

The 'Captain's Chair' is a replica of an original in the Athenæum Club in Liverpool

The central room, transformed from Ballroom to Reading Room

Above the doorway which once linked the two ballrooms may be seen the two-faced clock that still shows the time in each room

The glass dome, once raised on a shaft, that lights the central room

One of several doors that feature the egg-and-dart architrave moulding

Chandeliers and mirrors

View of the Mall Gardens from the Front Bar Room

Formerly the Coffee Room, this spacious room has become a bar and restaurant

A popular corner of the front room

A serving dish from the Clifton Grand Hotel, as the Club premises were once known, showing the façade before the alterations took place

Presented to the Club in 1858, this weighing machine was judiciously placed near the refreshment room

Postbox for members' mail

An example of Victorian comfort and elegance

unasphalted roads was likely to send the rider flying through the air in the most undignified fashion. 'Cropper' and 'crowner' were terms especially coined for these falls, which inevitably marked the victims with cuts and bruises, while sometimes they were fatal. Danger signs at the top of hills reminded riders that it was advisable to dismount and walk; anyone venturing to coast down a hill was advised to hang his legs over the handlebars, in order to be thrown clear when the anticipated accident occurred. Instructions on how to fall were included in cycling manuals of the time:

> A fair fall on the road. especially if the shoulder can be made to come first to the ground, generally results in a series of somersaults, which is nothing like so dangerous as a dead stop against a bank or wall. It may seem absurd to offer hints on how to fall, but it is quite an art of itself, for which many riders develop a peculiar talent.

There was a further danger in the form of professional coachmen, who could be tempted to use a whip and lash out at figures perched on high-wheelers that overtook the time-honoured horse with such ease.

It is difficult to imagine that any member of the Clifton Club would have invested the considerable sum of £12 in one of the tall, unstable penny-farthings, risking unavoidable croppers as well as ridicule from ordinary pedestrians. There would have been too much prestige at stake. And yet, by the mid-1870s there were fifty thousand such vehicles in England, manufactured by at least thirty different firms. In 1877 the *Daily Telegraph* pointed out that this was no transient fashion:

> Bicycling is a healthy and manly pursuit with much to recommend it, and unlike other foolish crazes, it has not died out.

For an adult to learn to ride such a heavy, unwieldy machine, it was essential to attend one of the special schools where graduated half-hour lessons cost in the region of 1/6d, with riding guaranteed at half a guinea. Once he had learned to control the mechanism, while maintaining his balance astride the tall wheel, a rider could achieve exhilarating speeds of up to twenty miles per hour.

Prosperous Victorian businessmen with a sense of adventure would have chosen a more stable form of transport — the tricycle, favoured by Queen Victoria and other crowned heads of Europe. As the choice of better-bred persons, it was not prone to sudden accidents. Many varieties of tricycle were available during the 1880s, including some which carried goods, and a number of these must have been seen on the streets in Clifton. It may be assumed that some avant-garde Club members favoured this form of transport.

During this decade, the penny-farthing was modified and became accessible to a much wider section of the respectable public. The solid iron frame was now hollow and wheels of equal size were cushioned by pneumatic tyres. This new chain-driven safety bicycle was lighter in consequence, bouncing over obstacles instead of throwing the rider off. By the 1890s the bicycle revolution was in full swing. At this stage, certain intrepid members of the Clifton Club chose to join the cycling fraternity. Their number increased with the escalating bicycle boom which, by 1895, was transforming the routines of daily life for one and a half million people in Britain.

There was now an unprecedented problem at the Club: where to accommodate the machines that members were so anxious to bring inside the building? Expensive toys, often personalised to suit the owner's status, they were lovingly looked after and would normally be kept in bicycle stands — which were taken for granted, even in the most impressive entrance halls. Not so at the Clifton Club, however, where the Committee's first reaction was to ban all bicycles from the premises. The Secretary was directed to put up a notice to this effect, while the hall porter was authorised to call members to order should a bicycle cross the threshold. For the following six months, all such machines were left on the pavement outside — until it was again proposed that they might be allowed on the premises. Very reluctantly, the Committee yielded, but they felt unable to provide stands in full view.

> It was resolved that arrangements be made experimentally for one month to allow members to put their bicycles in the inner lavatory, on the understanding that the Club property was not damaged and the services of the servants not employed in this work.

Was this the beginning of democracy and DIY? Unlike horses, which could be passed to a groom after use, bicycles demanded their owners' personal attention in matters of parking and maintenance.

The experimental parking scheme worked so well that it became permanent. However, the Committee did object to the way bicycles were left anywhere but in the stands provided — and the fact that some members who arrived on two wheels returned home by other means. The Minute Book of 1896 records that:

> As much inconvenience had been caused by members leaving their bicycles in the Club all night, it was resolved that a charge of 6d be imposed for bicycles so left.

The new regulation produced a good revenue over the following fifteen years without altering the members' habits in any way. A little more lenient by 1911, the Committee resolved 'that Members be allowed to leave their bicycles on the premises one night only per week without a fine'.

As more and more people learned to balance

successfully on two wheels, the cycling craze spread to most social strata. The bicycle — originally that gravity-defying miracle — would soon be taken for granted and lose its élitist appeal. It was to be overtaken by a far more exclusive mode of transport.

Horseless Carriages

During the last two decades of the nineteenth century, the horseless carriage was being developed, thanks to Benz and Daimler, whose experiments with the internal combustion engine had produced something which could be incorporated in a primitive motorised vehicle.

As expensive playthings for the wealthy, these devices were rarely seen on the roads in Britain, due to the short-sighted 'Red Flag' Act which stipulated that a man on foot should precede any motorised vehicle, effectively restricting speed to four miles per hour! Prior to that, a limit of seven miles per hour had been set for the steam-driven coaches that ran regular services between major English towns on the newly-constructed roads in competition with the railways. The stipulation that motorised vehicles should travel at walking pace not only brought about the sudden decline of the steam coach; remaining in force for twenty years, it delayed Britain's participation in the new motor industry that was rapidly evolving on the continent.

The Emancipation Act of 1896 finally raised the limit to twelve miles per hour, and horseless carriages appeared on British roads. A few may have been seen in Clifton, beautifully finished by a coachbuilder and steered via a curved bar or vertical handle. Every vehicle was uniquely customised, using techniques from the horse-drawn era, since the new transport was considered as just a deviation from normal carriages. By the turn of the century, the general specification of the motor car had been established and major technical problems corrected. Although a few steam-driven and electric cars existed, petrol had emerged as the favoured fuel.

Edward VII lent some impetus to the new industry when in 1902 he acquired the first motorised conveyance for the royal family. Admittedly, this was a Daimler from the Continent, but his patronage promoted motoring and encouraged the wealthy to place orders with the few British firms producing chassis. Each chassis purchased would be passed on to a team of specialist craftsmen for personalised completion, after lengthy consultations. With style as a central issue, a great variety of coachwork designs appeared and cars began to lose the motorised-carriage look.

The Thousand Mile Trial would certainly have introduced some of the many different types of car to people around Britain in 1905. Bristol was one of the first stops on the route from London to Edinburgh and back. Its inhabitants would have been amazed to witness the stream of Edwardian vehicles passing through at the new speed limit of twenty miles per hour. It was this limit (maintained until 1930) that discouraged the long-distance racing so popular in France, where motorised transport was more advanced as a result of constant competition. The American car industry was also well ahead, specialising in large-scale production methods before the turn of the century. These kept prices down and made cars available to the middle-class owner.

In the early years of the twentieth century, various

members of the Clifton Club would have succumbed to the motoring vogue, possessing open-topped cars with low horse-power: names like Napier, Riley, Wolseley, Lanchester, Humber and Sunbeam come to mind. By 1914 the motor car had developed from a toy for rich enthusiasts to an accepted element of everyday life. Unfortunately, this steady progress was now paralysed by the First World War, and did not resume for five years.

After the war it became obvious that taste had changed. The technical evolution of the Edwardian vehicles had laid the foundations for large-scale production and design in the twenties. It was vintage cars of this decade that were acquired by a substantial proportion of the Clifton Club members. Some employed chauffeurs, who took responsibility for the vehicle in the owner's absence, while others drove themselves. The notion of leaving expensive motor cars untended in the streets did not appeal to early motorists — hence the invention of car parks, which offered a measure of security at least.

By the thirties, the Club's many car-owners were experiencing some of the earliest car-parking problems to be documented in Clifton, chiefly due to the sensitivity of residents in West Mall and Caledonia Place. The car park in that area was intended for the general public, most of whom removed their vehicles before the small hours, while Clifton Club members did not. In spite of reminders displayed in the Reading Room, members seemed unable to get themselves home either quietly or early, but regularly woke the irate neighbours. Emerging noisily from the Club premises well after midnight, they used the starting handle on each car before roaring off in different directions — an unprecedented disturbance at that time!

In November 1933, after a letter of complaint had been received from the Mall Green Committee, it was resolved to invite its Chairman to attend the next Committee Meeting and express his views. Two weeks later, the invitation was taken up:

> Mr Lawes on behalf of the Mall Green Committee addressed the meeting at length, setting forth the inconvenience that the residents in West Mall and Caledonia Place were experiencing owing to the vicinity of the Car Park and made various proposals as to remedying this inconvenience. After full discussion, the Secretary was directed to write to Mr Lawes to the effect that the Committee, whilst only too ready to assist him in any attempt to keep the Park as quiet as possible at night time, felt that they were in duty bound compelled to resist the imposition of any limitation to the freedom of the Park as it then existed.

It appears that the Town Clerk was persuaded by Mr Lawes to intervene on behalf of the residents and close the Car Park. A notice on 'the New Regulations Regarding Car Parks' was posted at the Club. Further letters arrived from Mr Lawes, this time 'complaining of the noise made by members on quitting the Club' but, somewhat impatient by now, the Club Committee decided to take no action. Free parking facilities were offered by the sympathetic management of Clifton Down Hotel (situated in nearby Sion Place), where unfortunately cars could only be accommodated in the day-time. Although the Committee resolved to approach the Town Clerk in the hope of getting the local car park reinstated until 9pm, we may assume that the petitions subsequently drawn up came to nothing, as there was still no change two years later.

This prolonged argument was finally settled in 1939 by the petrol shortage and blackout conditions, which restricted motoring. Nocturnal disturbances experienced through the war years were far worse than any noise caused by members returning home from the Clifton Club. In fact, the Mall Green Committee might well have preferred the sound of friendly voices issuing from the Club to the warning howl of sirens and bombs crashing on the city.

17

Food and Drink – Nineteenth Century

How many gentlemen's clubs have been fortunate enough to have direct internal access to a tavern actually on the same premises? Such a mutually beneficial arrangement was enjoyed by members of the Clifton Club for the first twenty years of its establishment in the Mall. As the Committee's chosen tenant, the landlord of the Shades was quite amenable to devoting the first floor of the tavern to the needs of members, while the general public had access from Waterloo Street to the Tap, at ground floor level. In the original plans for converting the Royal Hotel into Public Rooms, a Refreshment Room was situated on the first floor adjacent to rooms occupied by the in-house Tavern, whose landlord would be expected to supply members with refreshments of all kinds.

It is easy to visualise this room with its original good quality carpet 'of a mixed Turkey pattern', upon which stood mahogany tables with stained deal tops (costing £3.15.0d each) and a dinner wagon three feet wide (at £16). The second landlord, Mr Hooper, agreed to supply plate, linen and tableware for the Refreshment Room, which he would also run. But the drawbacks were daunting:

> Mr Hooper stated that in consequence of the kitchen being filled with rubble etc he was prevented making use of it for cooking purposes.

When this was pointed out, the Committee resolved to clear the kitchen and supply dressers. Cooking would have been done on a range hotplate, had this been in working order. (It is interesting to note that the landlord of the Tap and Shades had no sink or running water in his own domestic kitchen in Waterloo Street until 1861, when water was first laid on.)

Mr Hooper enjoyed 'the privilege of supplying refreshments to the Club' from his primitive kitchen for almost a decade. As standards deteriorated over the years, the members became increasingly critical and the unpalatable catering was the subject of a petition signed by twenty-three of them in 1869. An accompanying letter complained of the food, wines and spirits supplied by Mr Hooper 'as being of a very inferior character and requiring the interference of the Committee in the matter'. On being summoned to attend their next meeting,

> Mr Hooper stated that he paid for the sherry supplied to the members at the rate of £20 the quarter cask, that the brandy was Hennessy's and the food of the best description he could procure. The Committee considered, having examined the invoice, that the sherry was of an inferior class and was not the wine which Mr Hooper agreed with the Committee to supply to the Club... Mr Hooper was referred to the covenant contained in his lease whereby he agreed to supply the Club with refreshments to be approved of and determined on by the Committee, and he promised that in future the quality of the wine should be improved and that he would do all he could to satisfy the members and the Committee with respect to the

refreshment furnished at the Club.

On the basis of this undertaking, the Secretary was able to reply to the petitioners:

> The Committee have considered the allegations contained in the Memorial and have examined Mr Hooper thereon, and they hope from what has taken place and the promises made by Mr Hooper that in future the character of the refreshments will be improved to the satisfaction of the Members and any grounds of complaint will be removed.

There seems to have been little improvement, however, as shortly after making these promises Mr Hooper was given notice to quit, with which he gracefully complied.

Arrangements were made to reinstate the previous landlord, Mr Pomeroy, for an interim year, after which followed a succession of seven landlords, all of whom were rapidly disillusioned and withdrew one by one.

In 1873 the Refreshment, Card and Smoking Rooms all exchanged function. New carpets were ordered from Kidderminster for these rooms and it was hoped that general improvements would result from the refurbishment. Nothing changed, however. The local press commented on the AGM held in March 1874:

> Mr Tovey made some few observations as to the defects in the cuisine and liquor departments... Strong complaints were made as to the manner in which the cuisine was carried on. He perceived by a bill in the room that they could supply 'Melton pork pies', which were no doubt very good, but he also understood that members who wished to have brandy with their pies must carry it with them in their own flasks if they wished to have that which they could drink with comfort (laughter). He thought something should be done towards improving this department, for there was certainly room for improvement. The Chairman said the cuisine had always been a thorn in their sides, and five or six persons had undertaken it at different times, but they all failed to give satisfaction. The truth was there was very little refreshment taken in the Club, and it was not worth anyone's while, nor would it pay them, to devote special attention to it, unless security could be given that a certain number would

> dine or lunch each day. It had been tried, he believed, in the Clifton Down Hotel, where a number of gentlemen met, but they were informed that, unless a receipt of £200 to £300 a year could be secured in that department, it could not be continued. Colonel Hume said that the question of the cuisine and supply of wines and spirits had received great consideration by the Committee but it was impossible with the means at their disposal, to give the satisfaction they would desire to give.

The Committee was forced to make new arrangements in 1875, when the police ordered that all internal communication between the Club and the Tavern should cease. A Wine Committee was immediately appointed to ensure that members did not suffer, but it seems that catering facilities came to an abrupt end.

The Old Coffee Room apparently lacked a function after 1875 and changed name in 1881, becoming the venue for future Committee Meetings. When the Clifton Club Company took over the running of the Club the following year, Dr Marshall gave an outspoken address at the AGM, nostalgically recalling the convenience of the original Refreshment Room:

> Far from there being any improvement in the character of the Club since it was established twenty-five years ago, it had rather deteriorated, and they now missed accommodations which they then possessed; for they then possessed a convenient dining room and a good cook and could get a comfortable meal on the premises, but dining room and cook had long disappeared.

Five years later, catering arrangements at the club seemed to be nearer realisation, when Ghent and his wife were engaged respectively as head servant and cook at a combined wage of thirty shillings weekly. In the event of dining arrangements being completed, the couple were to be boarded in a furnished house and Mrs Ghent would receive a maximum of £20 per annum for her services in the kitchen.

It was not long before light refreshments again became available at the Club. The Sub-Committee responsible suggested that the Committee Room be used as a temporary Coffee Room on an experimental basis, and that an initial outlay of £50 be sanctioned. Plain dinners, luncheons and light suppers were envisaged at a price between three and five shillings. The kitchen and cooking equipment were to be located in the house which the Ghents occupied in Waterloo Street, while waiting could be included among the duties of servants already in the Club's employ.

To the satisfaction of the members, who had by now been deprived of in-house catering facilities for twelve years, arrangements were running smoothly within weeks:

> The Sub-Committee appointed to provide light refreshments in the Club have received considerable support during the last six weeks, and believe that members have found the temporary Coffee Room a great convenience. They have been confirmed in their view that feeding arrangements at the Club can be carried on with little or no loss to the finances of the Club, and that considerable profit may be made from increased consumption of wine etc. The Sub-Committee ask that they may be permitted to continue the present Coffee Room for two months, and that they be authorised to pay a cook a salary not exceeding £2 per month for such time and to engage a Coffee Room Waiter at not exceeding twenty shillings per week.

The experimental resurrection of the Coffee Room had been so successful that the next step was to reinstate the former dining facilities. In 1889 a large table cloth was purchased (at fifty shillings) with enough crockery for twelve diners. A set of fish knives and forks was presented by Mr Nash and gratefully acknowledged by the Committee. Having lacked a dining room of any kind for so long, members were most appreciative. At the AGM of 1889, it was announced that in a year they had consumed a total of 2,103 meals on the Club premises, and that most gentlemen had chosen evening meals in preference to lunch.

The Committee did its best to maintain law and order in the new Dining Room. A notice was pinned up outside the door requesting members to inform the staff in advance if they intended to dine at the Club. Another notice inside reminded them that payment was required. A third notice asked members to write all complaints on the reverse of their bills for the attention of the Committee. And a new rule permitted the invitation of outsiders:

> All elected members have the privilege of introducing guests to lunch or dinner; such guests shall have the entry of all the Club Rooms whilst in the company of the member inviting them, who shall be held responsible for their conduct in the Club.

While there is no record of unacceptable conduct on the part of any guest, numerous instances of misconduct can be traced to the butler, Ghent, whose impertinent repartee provoked letters to the Committee from several members, General G Davis being one of the first.

The Secretary was directed to convey regrets of the Committee to General Davis at the annoyance he had received and also to inform him that Ghent had been severely reprimanded and cautioned that, should another complaint of the kind be received, he would be instantly dismissed.

The following year, the temperamental butler and cook gave their notice, but withdrew it within days. Ghent was summoned to a Committee meeting:

> The Chairman explained the terms on which he was allowed to remain, when he gave his assurance that the Secretary should not have cause again to complain of his or his wife's conduct.

Despite the butler's unfortunate manner and the fact that members often neglected to pay their bills, the Dining Room first began to show signs of profit in 1894, when it had been established for five years. This happy state of affairs persisted and, although the servants and all Ghent's children were receiving free board, a substantial profit was subsequently noted. To keep costs down, there were no sweets on the menu, which remained simple and homely, though luxuries like venison were sometimes available. The gift of half a red deer by the Duke of Beaufort would

obviously have had a beneficial effect on finances at a time when the Committee was struggling with an adverse balance. On being asked to submit a report on the management and financial condition of the Dining Room, the Dining Sub-Committee gave a very positive account of the progress made.

When the catering facilities were restored in 1885, Messrs John Harvey & Sons offered to keep a cellar on the premises for the benefit of members, and the understairs storage area near the Coffee Room was converted for their use. Nine years later, the Committee approved Messrs Harvey's plans for altering and reorganising this cellar, providing the Club were put to no expense in the matter. To ensure maximum profits, members dining at the Club were not allowed to bring their own wine; instead, such palatable wines as Krug and Pol Roger were provided by Harvey's. The Committee must have been satisfied with the revenue from the bar, since a momentous decision was made, reducing the amount realised by a bottle of whisky to five shillings by increasing the amount of whisky in a 6d measure.

Harvey's wines enhanced the Ghents' catering service, which was appreciated by members for a period of eighteen years. This came to a sudden end when Mrs Ghent wrote the following letter to the Chairman in 1903:

> Dear Sir
> It is with the greatest possible regret I am sending in my resignation, but as I am much worried about my private affairs I feel sure I should be better out of this kind of situation.
> Thanking you for all your extreme kindness to me, I remain Sir,
> Yours most respectfully
> E Ghent

The Committee called upon the butler to resign with his wife, and the Dining Room was closed until a new cook had been appointed. As might be expected, Ghent's departure was turbulent. When he failed to hand over the stock of spirits and cigars, it was found that he owed the Committee £9.7.0d. Ghent, instead of settling his debts however, belligerently maintained that the Club owed him £5.11.0d and engaged Mr Treasure, a solicitor in Gloucester, to represent him in the County Court. Messrs Stanley Wasbrough & Doggell advised the Committee to try to reach a settlement without a court hearing. This was achieved when Ghent offered to resign his claim if the Committee would agree to abandon their claim against him — which they did, for the sake of expediency.

18

Food and Drink – Twentieth Century

After the traumatic departure of Ghent and his wife in 1903, it took almost two years for catering at the Club to return to normal. The Committee eventually resolved that 'when possible, soup and a chop be served in the Dining Room if notice be given by 6pm, the charge for same to be 2/6d and 6d table money'. The later purchase of a stock of china to the value of £11 and six dozen table napkins at £13 would seem to indicate that things were running smoothly again — so smoothly in fact that no confrontations with the new butler and cook have been recorded.

Meanwhile the bar continued to make a steady profit, which meant that prices could be kept to a minimum. By 1909 the price of whisky had been maintained at 6d per measure for eighteen years, and it was decided to increase this by one penny. The price of brandy was also to be raised slightly to 5d per measure. At this stage the Committee, who had misgivings about the quality of the whisky supplied by A L Clarke & Co of St James's, asked for a guarantee that the Club was receiving eight-year old pure malt whisky. While it was no guarantee, the following extract from the supplier's letter may have dispelled their doubts:

> Stirling is a blend of malt and grain, and whilst we can guarantee its age as being quite eight years, we would point out that some of the whisky used in the blend is not of that age whilst some is much older. The greater part of the whisky used in the blend is 1898 whisky. We might mention that pure malt whisky is used for blending purposes, and is very rarely drunk for itself being of too pronounced a flavour.

Beer was also served at the Club. It was supplied in four and a half gallon casks by George's (at 4/6d) and Ashton Gate (at 6/-), while Anglo Bar cost as much as 7/6d per cask. When Mr Harvey complained that Barclay's lager beer was not up to standard, Graham's lager beer was substituted.

The First World War completely disrupted the comfortable routine of the Club, not least in the Dining Room and Bar. By 1918 whisky was in such short supply that the Committee decided to ration consumption to one bottle of that elixir per day. Another wise decision was to invest £110 in the contents of Harvey's cellar, which were still on the Club premises. To encourage members to order the more easily obtainable soft drinks, barley water was introduced (at 2d per glass), and effervescent drinks became available when the Committee expended £10 on a sodastream outfit for the

Bar.

The war over, it was time to re-establish the Dining Room yet again, and the following letter was addressed to every member:

Dear Sir,
In accordance with the resolution passed at the Annual General Meeting of the Club held April 29th 1919, when it was decided to re-open the Dining Room, I am directed to inform you that from October 25th a dinner consisting of soup, fish, joint, savoury and cheese will be provided nightly at a charge of 5/6d for members and 6/6d for guests. Members requiring dinner must give notice of their intention to dine not later than 4 pm.
H Reid, Secretary

The restoration of dining at the Club was much appreciated by members, who supported the Dining Room sufficiently to produce a small profit, despite wages for the increased staff. In 1921 Mr G H Beloe proposed a revolutionary plan for making the Dining Room really successful as a financial venture: the experimental introduction of lady guests on Tuesdays and Fridays. The arrival of any such guest would be announced twenty-four hours beforehand, when the hall porter would enter her name in a register.

The proposal was carried unanimously. However, at the following Committee meeting, three weeks later, there had been a change of heart. Enough time had elapsed for serious misgivings to be expressed and as a result the resolution was unanimously rescinded, another example of the remarkable unanimity of this Committee. Gentlemen-only dinners continued throughout the twenties, the House Dinners being well-patronised, lively events which involved keeping the Club open well beyond the usual closing time of 2am. When numbers became excessive — as for example at the Billiard Handicap Auction — the Clifton Caterers Company was called in to prepare and serve meals.

The American Bar

The original Dining Room, which had been converted to a second Billiard Room in 1924, was commandeered ten years later for a Lounge Bar, in which a curved counter seemed to be an essential feature. Messrs Cowlin accepted the commission to redecorate the present Bridge Room and build a counter in the shape of a semi-circle (with foot-rail), in keeping with the prevalent style of the thirties.

At the Clifton Club, where the functions of the various rooms were altered regularly, the servants changed rôle with similar ease. Accordingly Rapps, who had proved completely inefficient as a billiard marker, was put in charge of the Bar and Lounge. In the autumn of 1933, the fashionable Cocktail Bar was eventually opened. There was some danger that this would distract members from the sandwich lunches and cooked dinners provided, and a notice was pinned up by way of reminder:

> Now that the American Bar is opened and dinners served on all weekdays, members are requested, so far as conveniently possible, to partake of their refreshments in the upstairs rooms and so encourage the social life of the Club.

Bottles were kept cool in the ice-chest by means of a bar of ice, delivered daily. This had been the only method of refrigeration since the Club was first opened in the early nineteenth century. A note in the minutes book for 1913 mentions the investment of £9.15.0d in a replacement ice-chest — which was still in use in the thirties. An electric refrigerator would have been a useful gadget to install in conjunction with the American Bar, but when Prestcold Ltd offered to do this, the Committee declined. Finding that the ancient institution of the ice-chest was adequate, they uncharacteristically failed to see the wider potential of the electric refrigerator. It was not until 1950 that the subject was raised again, and this time Prestcold were gratified to receive an order from the Club for one of their refrigerators. In company with certain other modern inventions, the concept of domestic cold storage units — considered essential today — was greatly retarded by the Second World War.

19

Having a Ball

The Assembly Rooms, built as the principal venue of the local gentry and affluent visitors to Clifton, contained a most elegant ballroom. Ironically, this has become the central room of a gentlemen's club to which ladies are rarely admitted today. When the Club premises were first acquired in 1855, it took some years to alter the habits of local people, who obviously remembered the well-proportioned ballroom where major social events had taken place for over forty years. Very occasionally, the premises were still used for mixed social gatherings, culminating in the 1883 Ball given by the Committee to celebrate the completion of improvements to the building. It was forty-three years before the next occasion, when a Club and Hunt Ball was held there in 1926.

An alternative venue was provided by the Victoria Rooms, Charles Dyer's grandiose building in neo-classic transitional style, which was erected during the 1840s. It eventually diverted balls from the Clifton Club, allowing the ballroom there to take on a function more in keeping with a gentlemen's club and blend unnoticed with the rest of the building. So much so that when the Committee resolved to mark the Coronation of Edward VII with a magnificent ball, this was given in the Victoria Rooms.

The ball was planned for 8 April 1902. It was decided to issue five hundred tickets at one guinea each, four to be

The Victoria Rooms in Edwardian times

allotted to each subscribing member (two for gentlemen, two for ladies), with a further two available if required. For a total amount of £33, the Victoria Rooms were hired and the floor of the ballroom especially planed and sanded.

Hancock (the Clifton Club's main supplier of furniture and soft furnishings) undertook to decorate and furnish the areas to be used at a cost of £65. An elegant background was to be created by the discerning use of many rolls of fabric, both plain and of oriental design, which would curtain the windows, drape the doorways and festoon the walls. All corridors, steps and nooks were to be carpeted and decorated in style, so that no part of the main building was excluded from the festive transformation. Thanks to the installation of electric lighting, décor and guests would all be clearly illuminated.

In the ballroom itself the dado was covered with a plain fabric, above which contrasting swagging was relieved at intervals with large mirrors and superior prints. Against the soft lines and textures of this background, a profusion of plants was carefully arranged by the florists, Messrs W H Parker of the Royal Promenade, Clifton, whose bill amounted to £35. Three specimen palms were grouped in each window, in addition to the palms with a base of marguerites and genistas arranged round each of the three large mirrors. The unsightly hot water pipes along the walls were effectively concealed by the brackets of plants which they supported.

Two banks of palms and dracænas were used with striking effect on the platform, each group designed round a large square panel of arum lilies. Screening the front of the platform were tiers of white and yellow spring flowers and flowering plants, including azaleas, with yet more potted palms. Over the end gallery, which was swathed in fabric, grilled arches had been erected and draped. Beneath this gallery the impression of a sumptuous drawing room was created within tapestried walls, ornamented with mirrors and choice engravings. There were oriental carpets underfoot and a selection of easy chairs and loungers on which to recline. Cut flowers, foliage plants and ferns were deemed to be suitable as decoration here.

The *tour de force* was the ornate cascade of real water in the Octagon Room. This area was appropriately decorated as a winter garden and furnished in wicker and cane. Alongside the cascade itself were imposing banks of foliage and flowering plants, while generously distributed groups of mixed plants further contributed to the illusion.

Music being of supreme importance at a formal ball, the Committee selected carefully from a shortlist of five orchestras. In the event, the performers to be flanked by palms, dracænas and arum lilies were known as Iff's Band and based in Glasgow. The fee of £55 for the evening was to include all travelling, hotel and other expenses for twelve musicians, as well as the hire of a grand piano and the performance promised by Herr Oscar Iff. There were sixteen waltzes to be accompanied, two *pas de quatre*, two lancers and two polkas. These were neatly printed on the programme — a folded five-inch square with deckled edges, adorned with the intertwined C motif.

Superior catering was also essential at such an event. Without hesitation, the Committee selected Fortt & Son, of Regent Street, Clifton, and Bath, whose high standards and competence always ensured success. They agreed to provide such equipment as gas stoves, all necessary tableware, service and of course food for five hundred guests, at a cost of 7/6d per head. Their menu, printed to match the programme, was presented in (not quite perfect) French:

Olives Farcies
Amandes Grillées
Fleur de Lys d'Anchois
Consommé à la Royale

Mayonnaise de Saumon aux Concombres
Matelotte des Soles et Anguilles
Aspic de Crevettes

Hure de Sanglier au Chasseur
Dinde Farci à la Royale
Les Oeufs des Pluviers
Chaudfroid des Cailles
Médaillons de Volaille aux Truffes
Jambon de York
Langue de Boeuf
Côtelettes d'Agneau au Menthe
Paon au Naturel
Pâté de Foie Gras en Terrine
Chapons Découpés au Cresson

Salade Française
Salade d'Homard

Bavarois d'Ananas
Charlotte Russe Vanille
Crème aux Fraises
Gelée de Dantzig
Compote des Pêches
Pâtisserie Française

Dessert

On arrival, guests ascended the crimson-carpeted steps, passed through the Corinthian columns of the wide portico and were welcomed with tea or coffee. They were offered everything from fancy sandwiches to Neapolitan ices and petits fours throughout the evening — in addition to the splendid six-course meal served in the Supper Room. With such specialities as boar's head, plover's eggs, quails and peacock, it seemed that even the most discerning palates had been catered for. This sumptuous cuisine was complemented by the décor of the Supper Room; oriental fabrics were draped or festooned around the walls and crimson baize covered the floor, while palms were gracefully grouped at each end of the room. After a memorable evening, satisfied guests were finally despatched in the small hours with a cup of hot consommé.

Although the Secretary of the Clifton Club included all these details of organisation in minutes of the meetings preceding the Ball, the evening itself hardly received any written comment retrospectively. Fortunately, a descriptive article in the *Clifton Society* provides a more personal account by a journalist, 'Barbara', who had attended and clearly enjoyed the auspicious event:

> The much talked of Club Ball given by members of the Clifton Club took place at the Victoria Rooms on Tuesday night. Without making invidious comparisons, we may look upon it as the Ball of the season. Nothing could surpass the excellence of all the arrangements, the beauty of the decorations or the delight of dancing to such lovely music as our hosts provided. Iff's Band has enjoyed a high reputation for a long time, and on Tuesday night they played magnificently throughout the evening, with a spirit and dash that did much towards ensuring the success of the dance.
>
> The decorations were not only extremely pretty, but they were also very original. On entering the Octogon (sic) Room, few of the guests could restrain their expressions of surprise and admiration. The room as we know it had vanished, and its place was taken by a grotto, of which the scenery was painted in the most realistic manner possible, and completely covered the walls. In the middle of it a miniature waterfall flowed from the ceiling to the floor, the water meandering through ferns and

plants innumerable. Not only was the effect charming from a picturesque point of view, but it kept the atmosphere deliciously cool, and consequently the Octogon Room was one of the most popular resorts for the dancers in the intervals between the dances.

The other sitting-out places were equally well arranged. The long lines of chairs had disappeared for the most part and were broken up by palms, basket chairs and divans. The floors were carpeted with scarlet cloth, and careful attention had been paid to the question of lighting. Whilst the ballroom had plenty of light, in the sitting-out places it was subdued to a becoming softness. Several passages, not generally in use, were thrown open at the far end of the ballroom and were decorated with bunting and draperies of art muslin. In the ballroom itself, festoons of art muslin in shades of fawn and pale blue draped the walls and long mirrors that reflected back the gay scene. Moorish arches, painted white, took away the bare effect of the end gallery. The space beneath it was converted into a drawing room for the benefit of the chaperons. There were quantities of palms about everywhere, and especially in the orchestra which was banked up with them, except for a row of chairs placed behind the band, which commanded an excellent view of the ballroom and formed a very popular resort during the evening.

Supper was served in the lesser hall about halfway through the evening. That the menu included everything that could be desired goes without saying. Small tables to seat four or six people were scattered about, each one being decorated with

> baskets of roses and lilies or vases of daffodils. The light was somewhat subdued, which was refreshing to the eyes after the glare and heat of the ballroom, whilst the atmosphere was cool and pleasant.
>
> The dresses were for the most part extremely pretty, and many people seemed to have on new costumes for the occasion, which of course added very considerably to the general effect. The latter was in a measure detracted from through the fact that white was so largely worn. Every other dress seemed to be of white silk or satin and therefore the coloured costumes were the most noticeable.
>
> A tall girl looked extremely well in a vivid shade of blue satin. The tucked skirt had insertions of lace let into it between the lines of tucks, and the bodice was trimmed with folds of chiffon and lace. Pink embroidered chiffon over silk of the same colour suited its wearer admirably, and so also did grey crêpe-de-chine with an accordion pleated flounce headed with steel passementerie. An ivory satin with the skirt flounced almost to the waist had a pouched bodice with a quantity of chiffon about it, relieved with a bunch of pale pink roses. Another white satin dress was made with three flounces of satin to the skirt and a much tucked bodice trimmed with lace, chiffon and a chou of black velvet...
>
> Dancing was kept up with great spirit until the small hours of the morning, and the members of the Club must be heartily congratulated upon the complete success of their beautifully-given dance.

In organising this major society event, the Clifton Club had excelled themselves and created a precedent that would be difficult to match in the future. Similar balls were proposed for the month of April 1903 and 1906 but failed to arouse sufficient interest. It was not until 30 June 1911 that another such event was arranged, this time to celebrate the Coronation of George V.

As far as possible, the original format was followed. A ticket for £3.10.0d entitled members to invite two ladies and another gentleman to the Victoria Rooms, where Herr Iff's Band was again engaged to accompany dancing from 9.30pm to 3am and Fortts provided a similar menu. The total outlay for the Ball was £339.17.2d, which sum included the following items:

Hire of Victoria Rooms	*£32. 5.0*
Decorating ditto	*59. 0.0*
Herr Iff's Band	*65. 0.0*
Supper	*112. 9.3*
Stewards' Badges	*1. 2.6*
Wine etc (J Harvey & Sons)	*38.13.8*
Spirits, Mineral water, Cigars	*8. 8.7*
Wine Waiters	*1. 1.9*
Constabulary	*1. 1.7*
Commissionaires	*14.0*
Programmes	*2.18.0*
Printing	*3.13.0*
Hire of Piano (Duck Son & Pinker)	*1. 1.0*
Electric Bells	*1. 0.0*

Although this second occasion was also an outstanding success, the Clifton Club never held another ball at the Victoria Rooms. The early years of the twentieth century, with their accent on opulent entertainment and gracious living were brought to an abrupt end by the First World War, which completely transformed the social scene.

20

The First World War

In 1914, when summer was at its height, the world was shocked by news that the nations of Europe, one by one, were taking up the challenge of war. By early August, a few days after Great Britain had declared her intentions, a telegram was posted in the Reading Room at the Clifton Club; this appealed for contributions from members to the Prince of Wales' National War Relief Fund. At the same time, the Exchange Telegraph Company was enlisted to supply war despatches at a weekly charge of £1, and although this service was initially envisaged for just a few weeks, it was intermittently maintained throughout the First World War.

With a generosity inspired by feelings of patriotism, the Committee resolved to invite all Naval and Military Officers stationed locally to become honorary members of the club. It was thought that they would replace the proportion of members who were on active service and who were similarly absolved from the payment of subscriptions. These philanthropic gestures were later rescinded, however, when revenue from the remaining members sank to unrealistic levels.

> The Committee regret that, owing to the financial position of the Club, they are compelled to modify their resolution of October 21st 1914, admitting all Officers on active service as Honorary Members during the period of the war. They hope that Officers who are in Clifton on short leave will make use of the Club as Honorary Members. But when an Officer is stationed or resident here for a more or less lengthened period they trust he will join the Club as a Service Member, the subscription being one half that of Ordinary Members.

The war conditions also gave rise to unwonted expenditure. Not only was it thought expedient to insure the furniture of the Club against air raids but while several of the staff were on active duty, weekly allowances were made to their wives. The few remaining servants were encouraged to cover for their missing colleagues by a weekly war bonus of three shillings and the Club was closed earlier in the evening to decrease their working hours. In compensation for the extra outlay, small economies were made, such as using playing cards more than once.

Although the First World War caused hitherto stable prices to rise suddenly, the depleted staff continued to provide basic catering throughout the war years. The Club dinner was now charged at 3/6d, plus 6d table money, while tea with bread and butter was 8d. Even more indicative of a dramatic rise in the cost of living, the price of whisky soared to 10d per measure while brandy shot up to an unprecedented 7d!

Instead of running the catering department as before, the Committee decided to hand this over temporarily to the butler Rapps and his wife, allowing them to purchase provisions and take the profits — which may have helped to satisfy their urgent demand for increased wages. Provisions being so expensive, the catering soon dwindled to simple refreshments and dining at the Club became one of those regretted pre-war luxuries.

By the spring of 1916 the financial situation was so critical that the deficit of £455 required immediate action. The Committee appealed to the Clifton Club Company, who promised a handsome donation of £200, and a circular letter was sent to members inviting their voluntary contributions towards the Deficiency Fund. At the AGM of 1916, it was reported that:

> An appeal for extra subscriptions has been made and the result so far has been fairly satisfactory. The Committee feel that the current expenses cannot be further reduced and that the only remedy is a substantial increase in membership. They therefore appeal to each individual member to do his best to introduce at least one new member.

The Deficiency Fund seemed to be insatiable, however. The following year another donation of £200 was received from the Clifton Club Company, and a second circular was sent out, appealing to members to make up the balance. It was in 1917, when the deficit was high and subscriptions fewer than ever before, that the Club servants applied for an increase in their wages 'in consequence of the great increase in the price of food etc'. Despite their problems, the Committee generously agreed to an overall rise in remuneration of twenty-five per cent.

At the AGM of 1918 it was announced that the status quo had hardly changed:

> Your Committee regret that there is again a deficiency in the year's working of £225... The result of economies practised

would have shewn a further reduction in the deficiency but for the increased cost of nearly every item on the expenditure side. An appeal has been made to members to clear the amount.

These financial problems were potentially solved in June 1918, by a curious turn of events. The Committee received a letter from Colonel James of the Royal Flying Corps, proposing to take over the Club premises as accommodation for officers of the School of Military Aeronautics who were stationed in Bristol. A substantial rent was offered, together with compensation for possible damage to the premises at the end of the tenancy.

As the matter was urgent, the Committee decided to vacate the Mall building within a fortnight, moving the Club to no 15 Victoria Square. The Knee Brothers (housed in what is currently the Clifton Arcade) undertook to carry out the removal for £14.5.0d, efficiently assisted by the Club servants, who each received a gratuity of £1 for their labours. These costs were reclaimed from the War Office, who eventually responded with an amount of £300.

It was only a matter of months before the war was at an end. The Club premises were returned by March 1919 — not quite in their original condition, but a £50 cheque was offered for the restoration of furniture. The Secretary, who had successfully co-ordinated both moves, was presented with the handsome sum of £25 by grateful members. Hopeful of finally rectifying the negative balance, the Committee sent an account for £563.2.0d to the War Loss Commission.

As no work had been carried out on Club premises

since pre-war days, it was now very evident that a general repair and refurbishment programme was needed. The Clifton Club Company was once again approached for a contribution and magnanimously waived one year's rent, while members provided a sum of £526.13.0d. Meanwhile, the War Office was still deliberating on the payment of a total claim for £1,200 which was eventually settled in 1921.

To counterbalance the rising prices and increased wages, the cost of ordinary subscriptions was raised to six guineas. This did not deter would-be members, however, and by 1920 membership had risen by 25% from a very reduced level at the end of the war. The Club was about to embark on a period of prosperity in its newly-refurbished premises — which formed a reassuring oasis for those older gentlemen who felt wary of the alarming social transformation of the twenties.

21
Squash

Squash was derived from rackets, which was conceived in a debtors' prison in central London during the early years of the nineteenth century. A fast game played with a hard ball, it was evolved in the walled yards of local taverns by anyone with time to spare. Rackets spread across Britain in the following decades and its principles were eventually adopted in the United States, where they are still flourishing. On this side of the Atlantic, however, the game is only played by a minority nowadays.

Just before 1820, while still in its infancy, rackets mysteriously became a craze at Harrow School. Every house there could provide the basic court, since only two walls at right angles were required. As these walls frequently included windows, a soft rubber ball was used instead of the standard hard ball. Even less of a potential danger was the punctured soft ball or 'holer', which tended to slow the game down by squashing against the wall and momentarily adhering to it. Generations of boys developed the Harrovian variant of rackets, which began to assume a separate identity. The prototype of squash was taking shape. As it was slower, easier to play and required less space than rackets, the new game was at first considered to be just a substitute. As such, it remained in the shadows until the latter half of the century.

It was probably due to former pupils from Harrow that

squash courts began to be included in large private houses and gentlemen's clubs. The Prince's Club set the trend in 1853 by constructing a covered court, where all important matches were played. At Harrow, the game was officially acknowledged in 1864 when four covered courts were built there. Squash had made its debut as a game for the well-educated, prosperous minority. Rackets on the other hand, unlike its well-established American offshoot, had no more than plebeian status and lost its popularity as the larger courts fell into disuse one by one.

The London Bath Club replaced the demolished Prince's as centre for squash activities, producing the first British professional in 1912, followed by several international players. Rivalry between the West End Clubs was stimulated by the Bath Club Cup competition, instituted in 1922. Generally speaking, there was great diversity of court dimensions, equipment and even rules, until these were standardised in 1923. The game attained official status in 1928 when the Squash Rackets Association was formed.

Only three years later, a proposal to build two squash racket courts was received with much interest at the Clifton Club. Membership had reached a low level in 1932, and the Committee was looking for promotional ideas to attract younger members. It was agreed that these proposed courts should be leased from the Clifton Club Company, who made arrangements for their construction to be carried out by the builders Cowlin at a total cost of £2,600, including £175 for new bathroom accommodation at the Club.

In the vanguard as usual, the Clifton Club was one of the first in the provinces to emulate the London clubs by installing squash facilities. It was not long before a Challenge Cup had been donated by Mr Vaughan and lockers were being designed for the new dressing rooms. The project was completed within six months, having exceeded the budget by £280. Known as the game of the privileged minority — to be found typically in public schools and gentlemen's clubs — squash was now thriving at two appropriate establishments in the area, Clifton College and the Clifton Club.

This ambitious project marked the fiftieth anniversary of the Club's change of constitution in 1882, when it became a tenant of the Clifton Club Company. As profit would have to be generated in order to cover the lease, it was decided to hire rackets at a shilling per person, and charge ninepence for use of the baths, with a towel included. The annual charge for a locker was five shillings. One of the main problems was bicycles, which members tended to park in the new dressing rooms and bathrooms, as cyclists had done since the 1890s.

To launch the project, a professional exhibition match was played on the courts, preceded by a house dinner, but for some reason squash did not have the same appeal as billiards. Was the game too strenuous? Or the change of clothing too time-consuming? Barely two years after the squash courts were inaugurated, there was a notable decline in the number of members using them. This was thought to be partly due to the deplorable way in which visiting teams were entertained. (Let us hope that the Old Cliftonian squash racket team, who were invited to lunch at the Club, received better treatment.)

In order to increase the revenue from the hire of courts, it was decided that lady visitors should be encouraged. The Committee felt that the creation of a Clifton Ladies Squash Club with a minimum of twenty members, would help to solve financial problems — especially if they had no venue of their own. Such a club was obligingly formed within six weeks, during the winter of 1934, and this kept the courts in use with revenue flowing in again.

In theory, female players had been admitted to the courts since their opening, but only if they were relatives and resident in a member's household. As a result of a special request from the Squash Rackets Association, female spectators were permitted to watch the match against the Jesters' Club. However, the Committee refused to stretch the boundaries any further when the Ladies Squash Rackets Club requested permission to introduce male visitors to the courts — unless they were under the age of nineteen.

The admission of ladies to the Clifton Club was an issue upon which the Committee definitely lagged behind its London counterparts. Before the First World War, London clubs guaranteed peace and seclusion to members, although several offered facilities for lady guests as well. When the ordered social round of Edwardian England was destroyed in

1914, women were obliged to play a more active rôle than ever before, replacing the absent men in various capacities. In these new circumstances, many of the London clubs considered it unreasonable to deny them access. Facilities for lady guests were increased, while some clubs even extended membership to ladies. This was one London attitude which the Clifton Club — usually so quick to endorse new trends — refused to follow. Ironically, it was only to keep the squash courts profitable that ladies were permitted to infiltrate at all, and there was certainly no intention that the main building should be overrun.

When the Ladies Squash Rackets Club ventured to raise the question of using the changing rooms, the Committee at once rejected the idea of a female invasion of their headquarters.

> The Secretary was directed to inform them that the Committee was unable to find any accommodation suitable for a Ladies Changing Room in the Club, but would consider favourably any suggestion relating to a dressing room outside the Club.

By way of compensation, other requests were acceded

to: a Ladies Honours Board would be erected in the courts and a challenge cup (not to exceed £7) would be provided. Much later, after further reminders from the ladies, the Committee reluctantly agreed to hand over the locker room in the Squash Club as a Ladies Dressing Room — and their annual subscription was increased to two guineas in consequence.

Despite frequent bookings by the lady players, the squash courts were still not paying their way in 1938:

> It was found that an adverse balance, increasing yearly, of £200 to £250 had resulted. The lease under which the courts are held, dated 19 July 1932 and granted for 21 years, was examined and it was considered that the condition therein contained, whereby the Company retains the ownership of the freehold of the courts after the Club has paid off the cost of the freehold and the erection of the courts, is onerous and it is suggested that the Company be asked to agree to the following proposition:
>
> That the Company shall convey the property to the Club at any time when the Club shall so request on payment of a sum equivalent to the amount of the Debentures then outstanding. It was also suggested that the Bank might advance to the Club the necessary amount to pay off the balance of the Debentures. If this can be arranged, the Club Company should be paid off at once. This would result in a considerable saving of interest. The amount now due to the Club Company is £2,250.

Provided that their solicitors approved of the scheme, the Clifton Club Company agreed to sell the freehold of the courts to the Committee.

Any further plans were curtailed by the Second World War. One court was blacked out to allow for evening bookings, while the dressing room in the main building was taken over by fire watchers each night. When the courts at Clifton College were demolished during an air raid, pupils there had reason to be grateful to the Committee, who offered the use of the Club's squash facilities every afternoon, at sixpence per game per player. This must have compensated for the absence of several lady players, transformed to Wrens, Land Girls or other manifestations of women at war.

By 1947, when things were returning to normal, a

daring suggestion was put forward by the Ladies Squash Rackets Club — that on the occasion of matches, the showers and dressing room in the main building should be made available to them. This suggestion received no support from the Committee, who immediately proposed an alternative — to build a shower reserved for ladies at the courts and commandeer the professional's room as their dressing room.

Quite apart from fending off the Ladies Squash Rackets Club, the Committee had always found the running of the courts irksome. It was necessary to encourage outside bookings to compensate for the members' lack of interest and cover the cost of regular maintenance, involving planing down, sanding and even re-laying the floors. A minor source of irritation was that male members who did play would insist on changing into their squash shoes in the main building and walking over the road, in spite of large admonishing notices, with no thought for the floor surface of the courts. In 1956, the Committee entered negotiations to let the courts, but without success. They then considered abolishing squash membership altogether and sending out a circular to include the following:

> For a long time the Committee has considered the present Squash situation to be most unsatisfactory for all concerned. It has created a club within a club with many privileges debarred to Squash members. The original plan was to build the courts to attract younger members into the Club, and this is still the intention of the Committee.

Since the advent of leisure clubs, some specialising in squash, those potential younger members who might have been attracted to the Clifton Club courts have been adequately catered for. When the game became popular with a wider section of the population, it was clear that it could no longer be contained within public schools and gentlemen's clubs. As squash is not a game for the élite nowadays, the courts at the Clifton Club have become something of an anachronism.

Indeed, from their very conception in 1932, these courts were in the nature of a white elephant. Over the years, they have generated more expense than revenue and have failed to attract sufficient interest from members. Much thought has been devoted to finding a new function for the squash courts, including their disposal for residential units or conversion to a car park for Club use. Unless members are suddenly seized with enthusiasm, they will soon need to forgo the squash facility and give the courts a more valid *raison d'être*.

22
The Second World War

No sooner had British participation in the Second World War been declared than the Committee decided that honorary membership should be offered to all officers on the active service list. Recommended officials of the various ministries and departments transferred to Bristol should have the freedom of the Club until the end of 1939, thereafter paying an annual subscription of £1 for the duration of the war. As the telegraphic despatches (which had provided the latest news in the war of 1914-18) had now been replaced by wireless broadcasts, the Committee posted the following notice in the Club:

> A wireless set will be installed in the Dining Room, but Members are particularly requested to use it only for listening in to the News Bulletins and Announcements.

With evening meals suspended and almost a quarter of the regular members away on active service, the Club was quieter than it had been for many years and the familiar financial problems associated with wartime gradually reappeared. When Jess Barton and Silcocks were 'called to the colours' it was decided to rearrange the duties and hours of the remaining staff rather than find replacements (though Mrs Barton later took over the running of the American Bar).

A change in the Secretary's status provided a yearly economy of £150, when the office became honorary for the duration of the war, with life membership to compensate for the discontinued salary. Similarly, the squash professional was to have his retaining fee withdrawn, while being permitted to run a shop on the premises instead. To make up the inevitable deficit, members responded generously to the Committee's appeal for contributions to the Club's Sustentation Fund. Despite these measures, however, expenses continued to outstrip revenue — not least due to the rising cost of living, which meant that a weekly War Bonus of five shillings was paid to all those members of staff who were still at their posts.

On a material level, much rummaging took place in the cellars and the resulting 'old iron stoves and other scrap iron' were donated to the government for war purposes. To assist members in locating their blacked-out Club on moonless nights, the corners of the façade were marked with white paint. It was decided to cover the windows of the Front Reading Room with lace netting in addition to blackout curtains in order to protect members from possible splintering of the glass. As part of the special precautions taken against fire, the neighbours and tenants were co-opted to provide mutual assistance as voluntary fire-watchers. This nocturnal duty was carried out on a rota by the Secretary, stewards, local shop-keepers and several of the members — the front door of the Club remaining open at night to give access to the fire watchers' headquarters in the squash dressing room.

Although the municipal decision to erect an air raid shelter in the Mall Gardens was hardly popular, it seemed to be a necessity. While Clifton was not a target area for enemy action, it was close enough to the centre of Bristol to attract occasional hits. On the night of 7 May 1941, when incendiary bombs actually fell on the Club building, a heroic member and two of the stewards acted promptly to prevent a major conflagration. As a result, only minimal damage was caused — covered by a cheque from the insurance company for just £20.

By 1941, the ping-pong table and darts board from the upper rooms of the Club had been presented to the Officers' Mess RASC at Clifton College. Shortly afterwards, these upper rooms were let to Bristol Waterworks at an annual rent of £165. The Committee was certainly generous and public-spirited throughout the war years; gifts such as the picture of the 'Flying Boat *Clifton*', presented to the Club by the British Overseas Airways Corporation, bear witness to this.

As the war progressed and rationing was extended to clothes as well as food, it became necessary to take precautions against theft. When the back door opening onto Waterloo Street was left unlocked under blackout conditions, coats hanging in the vicinity tended to disappear, evidently helping to eke out somebody's clothing coupons. Possibly even more alarming was the thought of potential burglars enjoying the Club's stocks of wine, spirits and tobacco, which prompted the Committee to insure these for £800 at a premium of ten shillings.

War-Time Catering

Once again, catering was adapted to the rations available. The Food Control Officer would have liked to issue supplementary rations for the provision of fifty hot meals a week at the Club, but reduced staff felt unable to cope with preparation and serving. After some negotiation, the Chairman obtained a special licence, so that somewhat sparse teas were served throughout the war years. To celebrate the end of the war, members of every category were invited, with their wives, to a memorable Victory Tea Party held on the Club premises.

Although the reduced number of members had managed to subsist uncomplainingly on rather basic refreshments for six years, they were less tolerant of the drought in the bar, where the shortage of spirits with reputable labels (whisky in particular) caused more despondency than the lack of square meals.

War-Time Spirits

Stocks of alcohol must have been hard to replenish by 1942, when the Committee decided to ration members to three single drinks daily, ie one measure of wines and spirits and one pint of beer. A new 'No-Treating' rule further reinforced the hardship.

By 1944, the Secretary reported that whisky supplies were actually running short, only a hundred bottles remaining at the last count. With such a relatively grim outlook, it was agreed to release no more than five bottles daily — three to the American Bar and two to the Dispense Bar. An additional bottle of Irish whisky was allowed on Saturdays. By the end of the war, the voluntary ration consisted of four bottles daily, and it would take almost a decade before spirits (in every sense of the word) were back to normal.

Although the war was undeniably over, the situation had hardly improved by 1947, when it became necessary to declare Sunday as a day on which neither whisky nor beer could be supplied at the Club. As some of the members were extremely concerned about this ruling, the Committee received a suggestion that any day except Sunday should be observed as a 'Spiritless Day'. Obligingly,

> the Committee decided that Whisky would be served on a Sunday but no Gin, and that Gin would be served on a Monday but no Whisky.

This deprivation was fortunately not long-lived, thanks

to an improvement in the supply of gin. As a result,

> it was resolved that the normal quota of Gin could be supplied to members on a Sunday, an extra bottle could be supplied to Monday's quota, and that Gin could be made available on a Saturday morning till 1pm if required by members.

There was no such luck with the whisky, however, and in 1948 the Wines Committee recommended that Monday and Saturday should be 'Whiskyless Days' in order to conserve the stocks. Mondays and Saturdays proved so painful for members, that the Wines Committee was asked to look into the possibility of obtaining whisky from other sources than the authorised supplier — excluding the Black Market of course. They came up with a non-proprietary brand, Ben Lomond, which members considered better than nothing; a case was purchased at £32.10.0d for use on otherwise whiskyless days, and exempted from the No-Treating rule.

By 1949 the whisky reserve was so low, that further steps had to be taken. A non-proprietary brand of Irish whisky was to be served at all times at a price of 2/1d per measure — there now being twenty-one measures to the bottle instead of the generous ten which had prevailed at the turn of the century. Ben Lomond meanwhile had so much risen in the members' esteem, that the price had risen likewise to 2/8d per measure.

After this crisis point, the whisky supply began to flow again. Whiskyless days were abolished and a charge of two shillings per measure was generally adopted. With the situation almost back to normal by 1952, the Committee decided to clear the stock of Irish whisky, offering it at 1/6d. The favoured brands, McNish, Old Angus and Black & White, were now able to supply more than the necessary 124 bottles monthly, making it possible for the Club to issue four bottles daily while also building up a reserve.

In 1955 problems still persisted, and as a result yet another rule was introduced. The Bar should be run on the basis of three-day periods: a proprietary day, a Gilbey day and a McNish day, in that order. On hearing of the predicament at the Club, Harveys very generously offered assistance in the form of half a dozen extra bottles each month, so that the problem was eventually resolved.

23

Club Members

Thanks to the detailed accounts provided by the old minute books, it has been possible to discuss most of the peripheral aspects of the Clifton Club — from the architecture and refurbishment of the Mall building to its administration and the services available to members. As records of the day-to-day running of the Club, however, the minutes have much less to offer where the human element is concerned. It is in the correspondence, preserved over the years, that a glimpse of the members may be caught.

Generally speaking, the atmosphere of a Gentlemen's Club ultimately depends on the members. 'A club is a place where a man goes to be among his own kind', and selection of members is therefore of paramount importance. Although this seems to be self-evident, selection procedures have sometimes been less than discriminating, allowing the occasional eccentric to enliven an otherwise conventional fraternity.

At the opposite end of the scale is another type of problematic person. It was once said that it would be preferable for ten unobjectionable men to be passed over, rather than admit one terrible bore to a club. Regrettably, this idea has not always worked in practice, as most clubs contain a few members who contrast sharply with the majority. Since eloquence and wit are greatly esteemed in clubland and conversation is one of its most entertaining aspects, the presence of such members can have a very negative effect on the general ambience.

It is unlikely that the Clifton Club has ever admitted the kind of member described by the satirist, Theodore Hook, when clubs were in their heyday:

> In the first place find fault with everything and bully the waiters. What do you pay your subscriptions for but to secure that privilege? Abuse the Committee for mismanagement, until you get on it yourself — then abuse everybody else... Never shut the door of any room... When the evening papers arrive, pounce upon three... When there is a ballot, blackball everybody you do not happen to know... Always walk about the coffee room with your hat on, to show your independence and your respect for the numerous noblemen and gentlemen who are sitting at dinner without theirs... If it is a wet night, and you are without a cloak or a great-coat, take the first that fits you; you can send it back in the morning when it is fine. This rule equally applies to umbrellas.

At the Clifton Club, worse things had happened to greatcoats. Indeed, one had been 'mutilated' — and one wonders how — while hanging innocently on a peg. This schoolboy prank, perpetrated by a visiting baronet in 1888, was received with very bad grace by the owner, another visitor to the club, and generated a record amount of correspondence. Mr Arnott attempted to make amends on behalf of his guest:

> I only returned to Bristol last night and heard for the first time the serious manner with which an after-dinner joke perpetrated by my friend Sir William Williams has been looked upon by your Committee. As the introducer of Sir William Williams I am of course responsible for his actions while in the Club, and herewith beg to tender you and the members of the

Club my apologies for having unwillingly been the means of disturbing the harmonious feeling that has always existed there.

The baronet himself sent an admission of guilt:

In justice to my friend, and other members of your Club, I think it my bounden duty to inform you that I as an after-dinner joke mutilated a coat in the lavatory, which I need hardly say, I now regret having done so, and beg herewith to tender my sincere apologies to the owner and other members of the Club, on whom suspicion may otherwise have rested. I shall feel obliged by your conveying my apologies to the proper quarters, and I need hardly say that any reparation I can make, I will gladly do so.

For the member (a solicitor) whose guest had suffered from the greatcoat mutilation, the whole episode was beneath contempt and beyond restitution. Having received the letters of apology from the Secretary, he replied:

I am in receipt of your letter and enclosures, for which please convey my thanks to the Committee, but I am afraid I cannot comply with their request to lay the correspondence before my friend as I should positively be ashamed to do so. Both the gentlemen who have written to the Committee are pleased I see to designate this outrage as an 'after-dinner joke' and this expression is accepted or at all events passed unnoticed by the Committee. I can only say that a Club in which such 'after-dinner jokes' are permitted to be perpetrated with impunity will in my humble opinion have but a short existence...

Such were the dangers of allowing outsiders into the Club, that rules were fairly strict. Much difficulty was made about admission when a gentleman called for 'a short conversation' with General Davis in 1890. The General's remonstrances led to a new arrangement for interviewing visitors in the lobby outside the Dining Room. Two years later, however, there was a fundamental change of heart towards the admission of visitors:

> All elected members have the privilege of introducing guests to lunch or dinner; such guests shall have the entry of all the Club Rooms whilst in company of the member inviting them, who shall be held responsible for their conduct in the Club.

The kind of conduct that provoked a reaction from the Committee was most often observed in the Billiard Rooms. Here a member, overcome by emotion, could fling down his cue on the table and cut the cloth — such damage occurred frequently and would cost the perpetrator one guinea. Members of a different temperament would allow the arrears due for billiards to mount up until they suffered the ignominy of having their names posted as defaulters; if a debt remained unsettled, the Committee wrote to the recalcitrant threatening expulsion from the Club. Other more discreet gentlemen arranged to play against the marker and tried to avoid paying for the tables if they won.

A special meeting was called in October 1878 to investigate an unprecedented matter — a charge made against one of the members by the junior marker, involving 'improper conduct' in the Billiard Room. The Committee accepted this member's resignation from the Club 'on medical evidence with respect to his mental state and that he was subject to insanity'.

As a challenging game, billiards seemed to over-stimulate the production of adrenalin and generally bring out the worst in people.

Similarly in the Card Room, there were incidents which demonstrated an unwonted lack of control. In 1865, for example, Mr Rankin accused Mr St Croix of misconduct while at the whist table. This led to numerous letters of explanation, but the whole affair was eventually settled amicably. It was doubtless due to a sudden surge of adrenalin that Mr Randall managed to damage a newly recovered card table and no less than two packs of cards in a single evening! Dramatic disturbances occurred in the Card Room when tempers rose one Saturday night in 1868: Mr Formes subsequently wrote to the Committee, complaining of the ungentlemanly conduct and abusive language of others present at the scene — but this conduct and language seemed to be explained by a complaint from Mr Otter that 'Mr Formes was in the habit of interfering with gentlemen when playing whist and intruding his conversation upon them in an offensive manner'. The Secretary duly sent a letter of reprimand and we can only hope that Mr Formes mended his ways.

Warning letters were addressed to other members who indulged in abusive language on several occasions when passions had been stirred up in the Card Room. In this way some restraint was maintained over outbursts expressed in language which 'ought not to be tolerated in any club'. Mr Evans, whose name figures more than any other in the correspondence, was among the verbal offenders. When informed that such language could not be permitted in the Club, he responded:

> The complaint against me relates to an incident between Captain Horniblow and myself, when I admit having used language which was perhaps excessive and I regret having done so in the heat of the moment, although it was under what I considered severe provocation.

The Secretary replied that the Committee 'did not consider any provocation justified the use of such language,

and in the event of a repetition they would have to take most serious notice of it'. An interim measure was to discourage talking in the Card Room where matters could so easily get out of hand, and a sign was put up requesting silence.

Another misdemeanour in connection with cards was that members sometimes strayed from the Card Room to continue their game in the Smoking Room, thereby provoking their more law-abiding colleagues who respected the exclusive function of each room. The matter was usually reported to the Committee by Mr Rankin (who seemed to have an obsession with law and order) and the Secretary would be instructed to write and chastise the culprits. To little avail, however — the straying persisted. One night five members were discovered playing poker in the Dining Room and the Secretary wrote to each of them individually. Waiters were instructed to remind members of the rules whenever they were infringed. In 1911 the Committee was eventually forced to compromise with a new ruling on the Small Dining Room:

> This room may be engaged as a private room for playing any game of cards, subject to the bye-laws of the Club, by a party of members not less than six in number, who have dined in the Club the same evening.

Persuading the card- and billiard-playing faction to actually leave the premises at night was no easy task. Fines had been imposed on a rising scale, depending on the hour of departure, but this system did not deter the latest leavers. In desperation, the Committee ordered the circulation of a printed notice in 1877, pointing out that 1am was the normal closing time, except on Saturdays when the club closed at midnight.

> The Committee appeal to the good feeling of the Members who are in the habit of playing Billiards and Cards late at night, to allow the Manager to carry out the instructions he has received on the subject.

In 1887 the incorrigible late leavers produced a petition with numerous signatures:

> We, the undersigned Annual Members of the Clifton Club, are of opinion that 1am is a very early hour for closing the Club, and hope that the Committee will consider as to the advisability of keeping the Club open until 2am.

However, the Committee simply retaliated with a new system of fines: 2/6d after 1am, 5/- after 2am, £1 after 3am, and £2 after 4am. Late leavers responded by tipping the porters or stewards instead of paying their fines. In this connection there is an amusing story about a somnolent member who fell asleep in a remote corner of the Club and was not discovered until the following morning. The problem was that the Committee could not decide how much to charge him for being on the premises so many hours after closing time!

The Suggestion Book, provided in 1885, was not always treated seriously by members, but the Committee ensured that no-one got out of line without a severe comment. One member's suggestions (tactfully unclarified) were disposed of in the following manner:

> The Committee's views of the social amenities of club life differ so materially from those of Captain Little that they decline to consider his complaints. They would however suggest that Captain Little had better transfer his membership to some other club more in harmony with his tastes.

On providing a written apology, the Captain was forgiven. Really unforgivable offences were tactfully passed over in the minutes. 'The conduct of Mr Allen was considered...' Whatever had Mr Allen been guilty of on the night of 5 February 1910 to merit the Committee's demand that he resign membership of the Club? Possibly something even more heinous than Mr Bowen in 1887. This member had appeared at the Club on two consecutive days in a state of intoxication. The Secretary wrote to inform him that, if there were a recurrence, his membership would be forfeited.

The Dining Room was a frequent source of grievances, one of the most graphic letter writers being Mr Evans. In May 1894, he wrote to the Chairman describing a skirmish with the insubordinate head waiter, Ghent:

> On my way from the Whist Room to the Lavatory this evening I met Ghent the Head Waiter and immediately mentioned that I was going to dine here and received the prompt reply that there was no dinner for me as it had all been bespoke and that the tables were all taken up — the time, I should mention, was

> 7.10pm. I naturally remonstrated by saying that I understood there was house dinner, to which the Waiter replied in more moderate tones that as only two or three had lately been dining they had not provided much. I then said that he must get me something as I had counted on dining here and that, as I had found him only too ready to provide the excuse if I was after the time, I should on this occasion insist on having something. He thanked me for my nice way of putting it and asked me what I would have, at the same time saying that I could only have a chop or a steak and that I should have to wait until the other gentlemen had finished and fixed the time to eight o'clock, to which I agreed. At 8.10pm, having had no intimation of my meal being ready, I made enquiries and the Waiter, after I had sent him for the third time, got an answer fixing the time for 8.30pm, when I went into the Dining Room and eventually got served at a quarter to nine, my dinner consisting of a chop, potatoes and asparagus. I have also to state that, contrary to the Waiter's statement, there was an idle table in the room.

It would seem that the two protagonists — both of whom clearly enjoyed conflict situations — had this time met their match!

24

Gentlemen's Gentlemen

There is an amusing anecdote about a certain aristocrat of the past who, displeased with the service in his Club, flung the offending waiter through the nearest window. Then, feeling some remorse, he offered financial compensation. 'Put him on my bill' he said magnanimously. Although the story does not relate to the Clifton Club, it illustrates the potential hazards of a club waiter's job in the early nineteenth century!

As the century unfolded, successive generations of club servants seemed to become more aware of their rights and less concerned about the members' welfare. In fact, there are numerous instances of cheek in the final decades, mostly resulting in dismissal. The structure of society was becoming insecure, an alarming state of affairs for the Victorian gentlemen who frequented the clubs. The control of behaviour and language was essential to respectability. Losing control over servants endangered the middle-class lifestyle.

All this was very much in contrast to the reliable efficiency and polite manner of such a legendary manager as Mr Hartland, who succeeded the renegade Mr Mardon in 1858 and ran the Club admirably for fifteen years. This 'able and zealous officer' died at his post, to the great regret of the Committee, who defrayed the funeral expenses and offered the surviving widow a gratuity of £100 — to which members added 'the very handsome subscription' of £300. This was a substantial amount of money, equivalent to three years' wages, and bears witness to the great esteem in which Mr Hartland was held.

There seem to have been few problems with the staff while Mr Hartland was in charge, but after his demise, things got out of control. One of the earliest confrontations mentioned in the minutes was between, Mr Colthurst (Chairman) and a marker:

> The Committee being dissatisfied with the Marker's demeanour and conduct, he was at their unanimous request admonished by the Chairman and informed that unless he was prepared to attend to the Rules laid down for his guidance he had better look out for another situation, to which the Marker replied that he felt very dissatisfied with the place and would adopt the suggestion of the Committee.

As we have seen, numerous arguments originated in the Billiard Room, and it seemed that servants were just as prone

as members to surges of adrenalin. Consequently markers were often replaced at the Clifton Club. They worked a minimum of fourteen hours a day, the wage for a junior marker being 10/- per week, increased to 12/6d in the 1860s. Thomas Rowe, who lived in central Bristol, probably found it a long walk to and from the Mall. He lasted two months before disappearing without notice. This lad was succeeded by Roland Rugg, whose habit of giving short change was reported by Captain Sloper and ended in his dismissal.

Of all the Club servants it is the markers who figure most prominently. Maybe it was the long hours and periods of idleness that got them into trouble. Some of the senior markers, however, managed to retain their positions for years. There was Mr Drake for instance, who became so incapacitated by ill health that the Committee had to ask him to leave his post. It was resolved that 'in consideration of his long services the Manager be directed to pay him the sum of ten shillings per week for the period of ten weeks, when the payment is to cease'. No wonder that people remained in employment to the very end; the only alternative would have been the poorhouse. A short illness meant that wages were reduced by half for a fortnight, after which no provision was made. A longer illness gave grounds for dismissal.

As rôles were reshuffled in the Upper Billiard Room, Henry Tizzard joined the team of markers. It was soon reported 'that he was not attentive to his duties and that his manner was on many occasions insolent and disagreeable'. As a result, members were avoiding both the marker and the room over which he presided. Henry Tizzard was accordingly dismissed. He was followed by the head billiard marker, discharged for absenting himself without leave, added to other general misconduct.

By the 1880s, this revolution seemed to have spread to other categories. The Committee dealt with the insubordination of one of the waiters, Owen Giles. Resignations were received from the new hall porter and the head billiard marker. Commissionaire Hunt was dismissed for being twice inebriated while on duty. Waiter Cunningham lost his job through disobedience of orders. The hall porter, Dowdall, was dismissed as incompetent. Commissionaire Carter resigned, the sixteen-hour days proving too long. It was at this point that the butler Ghent began his downhill career at the Club — a master of impertinence, he managed to avoid dismissal for several years while causing universal irritation. Meanwhile, others employed continued to qualify for instant dismissal: the waiter Chidgey for bad conduct, page Worral for dishonesty, head marker Fletcher for misappropriation of billiard money, marker Neatham for misbehaviour... Generally speaking the staff seemed incorrigible and the Committee relentlessly sacked one after another.

Judging from contemporary literature, discontent was being expressed by servants all over the country in the 1880s. Domestic service was going through a period of transition in the nineteenth century, expanding to play an important rôle in the evolution of the new urban society. The middle classes had been enlarged by an influx of new industrialists who created a demand for servants, the symbol of their success. These positions were often filled by young folk newly arrived from farming backgrounds, and this expansion raised the level of friction as neither group felt at ease in the unaccustomed role. The new middle-class employers were dissatisfied with the deteriorating relations, partly provoked by their own attitudes. Gradually they replaced the extended family concept of domestic servants with a more business-like approach. By exercising their new social superiority, they emphasised the inferior station of their servants, who began to show resentment. Problems were intensified, particularly in Clifton, by the concentrated domestic service in the area, which provided opportunities for servants to exchange notes. In this way the blight spread rapidly.

Traditionally, the Committee had always treated servants with a paternal benevolence, while refusing to tolerate any indiscreet familiarity. In return, they were expected to behave with grateful deference and to obey orders. Their new attitude, both impertinent and unwilling, must have been very disconcerting to conventional Club members.

The fact is that until 1880, wages had progressively increased as the demand for servants exceeded the supply. Then the situation changed. When people in service began to compare their conditions with those of other workers, obvious reasons for dissatisfaction emerged. Legally, they had minimal rights. They worked on average around one hundred hours a week for a few shillings. Holidays were rare and unpaid, illness could bring working days to an end — and old age was usually not provided for. With the Victorian insistence on order and stability, a great deal was expected of domestic staff, whose responsibility it was to ensure that routines were infallibly maintained. Then the need to behave with propriety and refinement was an added strain on people from working class or country backgrounds. While previously they had seemed to accept their lot graciously enough, they no longer felt adequately compensated for the inconvenience of service and particularly resented the comparative lack of freedom.

On the other hand, service had its advantages, as residential work protected people from hunger and homelessness. The Committee doubtless felt that the board and lodging which they offered were superior to most and in no way justified problems created by staff at the Club. In addition, the specially made uniforms and livery with which staff were regularly supplied must have seemed like a generous supplement to limited pay — while also defining their subordinate place in the social order.

After the watershed of 1880, people in service all over the country increasingly looked for other occupations and a constant turnover in domestic positions resulted. This also applied to the Clifton Club, where discipline was becoming difficult to enforce by the mid-eighties. Hoping to promote better relations, the Committee issued a set of *Rules for the Regulation of the Servants' Attendance* — which today would be regarded as a joke:

1. The Committee expect that the Club Servants will be punctual in their attendance, but for the present will take no notice of any case in which a servant may be late in coming on duty by six minutes or less.

2. All cases in which a servant is more than six minutes late will be reported to the Committee.

3. Any servant who is reported as being late three times or oftener in one week will in the absence of satisfactory excuse be liable to a fine of one shilling.

4. Any servant who on any one occasion is more than twenty minutes late will in the absence of satisfactory excuse be liable to a fine of one shilling.

5. All fines levied under these rules will be added to the Christmas Gratuity Fund and distributed to the club servants in such proportion as the Committee see fit.

Indiscriminate tipping being strongly discouraged in the Club as an infringement of Rule 29, the Christmas Box Fund was the alternative system. Adopted in many of the leading gentlemen's clubs, this entailed entering voluntary donations in a book left in the Porter's Lodge. These would be assembled each December and distributed to the staff. While this system seemed fair and provided a lump sum when it was most needed, the willingness of servants may have been affected by the absence of spontaneous gratitude and tangible reward for effort. Perhaps it removed motivation. Club servants were known to be relatively poorly paid and a little indiscriminate tipping might have been a useful supplement to wages. This matter caused some dissension among members, many of whom would have preferred the spontaneous method of showing their gratitude.

While more important members of the staff were permitted to rent the small houses at the rear of the Club, others received basic board and lodging — the kitchen maids for example, whose earnings were £12 annually, plus £2 for beer and washing. In the 1870s the accommodating Henry Gentle agreed to work a sixteen-hour day (ie ninety-six hour week) for a weekly wage of £1. For waiting and general duties around the premises he was being paid an hourly rate of twopence halfpenny. But things were to improve slightly in the 1880s: for the first time, holidays were included in a contract. After a year's work, each servant would have the right to one week's holiday at a date to suit the Club.

At the turn of the century the Committee became even more considerate. When Queen Victoria visited Bristol on 15 November 1899 the Club was closed for two hours, specifically to give the servants a chance to see the royal retinue. On 27 June 1902 the Club was completely closed to mark the Coronation and give all the servants a holiday. Again in 1908, the Club was closed for the afternoon so that servants might have an opportunity to see the King and Queen in Bristol on 9 July.

Although the pattern of decline had been established in the 1880s, domestic service was still the largest employment sector in the early years of the twentieth century. Broader social changes meant that the decline continued, despite progressive legislation on such unprecedented benefits as old age pensions.

During Edwardian times, the number of people who chose service as an option diminished steadily. The significant turning point was the First World War, which struck a final blow to the institution of live-in servants when it became obvious that other occupations offered more freedom and better remuneration.

It was also the First World War that put an end to the strained relations and discipline problems where servants were still employed. Victorian ideals had by now been phased out, society was moving into a new configuration and, not least, national solidarity was required. It was now a question of mutual support. Like several dozen of the members, some of the Club servants were on active duty. They were not replaced — but weekly allowances were made to their wives, while the few remaining staff shared the extra work involved in running the Club. It would appear that the national crisis greatly improved collaboration between classes, as well as the general morale.

After 1918, positions for domestic staff could no longer compete with the new jobs in the urban economy. It was the end of an era — domestic service would not continue to be an integral part of the middle-class way of life. In this new situation, the number of staff employed at the Club was reduced. Although the servants who had been on active duty returned to their posts, new labour-saving devices made it unnecessary to employ so many people; a vacuum cleaner for example was acquired by the Club as early as 1917. Over the next few decades, relations between the administration and a more streamlined, motivated staff improved markedly. Their welfare received more attention and by 1952 a pension scheme had been introduced, among other benefits. Members have now become much more appreciative of those who run the club for them, using Christian names instead of the more formal modes of address current in the past.

Reciprocally, staff seem to enjoy working at the Club, happily carrying out their duties for many years. Sheehan and Ray for example, who ensured that the Club was competently run throughout the First World War, were still at their posts in the forties. This meant that they were also able to see the Club through the Second World War before retiring — after forty-six and forty-five years respectively! Nevertheless, the prize for the longest service must go to Jess Barton, who was appointed in 1933 and did not retire until 1995. With unique aplomb and competence he looked after members devotedly for an impressive total of sixty-two years!

25

Conclusion

Gentlemen's clubs have been available to the privileged for almost three centuries now. During the eighteenth century when the concept was new and full of promise, the cream of London society emerged from the coffee houses to found clubs in premises of their own. The movement gathered momentum throughout the nineteenth century and dozens more clubs were set up both in London and major provincial cities: a new fashion had been launched. In the early days political networking was facilitated by the formation of these select groups, but in due course the spotlight moved to the new professional, commercial, artistic and literary classes. Those fortunate enough to be elected to a club made maximum use of the facilities offered, while candidates hopeful of

election resigned themselves to years on a waiting list.

By the start of the twentieth century, this enthusiasm had begun to wane. The war years had a negative effect on club life. Inflation has been damaging. The international cuisine in countless new restaurants has tempted gentlemen away from their simple menus to something more exotic. Improved transport has encouraged people to live outside cities so that their clubs are no longer just round the corner — and this has made dropping into the club more of a challenge than a routine.

Indeed, clubs have become something of an anachronism in a welfare state. These selective institutions blossomed in a pre-democratic age when it was accepted that a select few should live in style while the rest of mankind struggled to survive. It now seems that the clubs themselves are struggling to survive. Before it is too late, something must be done to rejuvenate them — an infusion of new blood to stimulate a weakening circulation.

To admit all and sundry in a democratic manner would certainly defeat the object, since clubs were created by the privileged for the privileged. But it may be that membership categories should be altered to include certain people who are considered unclubbable at present; this might help to increase revenue — unless it caused existing members to withdraw their support by resigning. Improved finance would certainly help to keep the institution alive, but if it meant sacrificing quality to quantity the character of clubs would be radically altered.

An appraisal of the flourishing new London clubs reveals that they are intended for the contemporary élite (regardless of sex) who qualify by being stylish and successful while relatively young, and are largely connected with the media. This is a different kind of élite, but it produces the desired result. While the old established clubs tend to become emptier as the day wears on, the reverse is true of their modern counterparts. A major attraction is the gastronomic superiority, which ensures that these people of means and taste will congregate at the club rather than in nearby restaurants. The combined talents and animation of members attract other professionals of comparable standing, but to qualify for membership, standards are high. The essence of these clubs is exclusivity — as it was in the original London establishments — and this will almost certainly be maintained, whatever other aspects need to be modified.

To ensure that our existing clubs survive well into the future, it seems that we may have to adapt criteria for membership, club activities available, administration, décor and even atmosphere. The reader will probably find it difficult to visualise the profound changes that might become necessary.

Founder members of the first Clifton Club near Birdcage Walk had a similar problem: they could not envisage the addition of new members to their established number and allowed exclusivity to become such a priority that the Club was finally obliged to close down when that number diminished. Today the problem which looms over the Club is far more complex and its solution must lie in our ability to harmonise with the times.

Chairmen of the Clifton Club

1818	*Clifton Club Rooms established*
1818/19	Sir Richard Vaughan
1819	P Flannaghan
1819	C L Walker
1819/20	Vice Admiral Sotheby
1820/21	W Richardson
1821/24	General W Browne
1824/25	G Anstel
1825/27	Sir Richard Vaughan
1827/28	Sir Henry Nicholls
1828/29	G Walker
1829/30	Dr J New
1830/32	General Browne-Clayton
1832/34	C Payne
1834/35	J Yerbury
1835/36	J Cookson
1836/37	S L Harford
1837/38	S O Bigg
1838/39	C Vaughan
1839/41	J Cookson
1841/42	C Vaughan
1842/43	J Cookson
1843/44	M G H Ames
1844/45	C Payne
1845/50	*No minutes recorded*
1850	*Rooms sold (Birdcage Walk)*
1855	*Clifton Subscription Rooms Association formed (The Mall)*
1857/59	J Colthurst
1859/65	J Colthurst
1865/76	J B Burroughs
1876/82	Captain J S Warren

1882 *Clifton Club Company formed*

1882/85	Captain J S Warren
1885/88	Dr H Marshall
1888/90	E King
1890/92	F H Pellew
1892/93	Sir F Blackwood
1893/95	Major General Still T Lloyd
1895/98	H Marshall MD
1898/03	J Osborne
1903/05	Colonel J H Woodward
1905/07	Dr R Ogilvy
1907/08	A W Blake
1908/11	Dr R Ogilvy
1911/12	A C Douglas
1912/14	Dr R Ogilvy
1914/16	A W Blake
1916/21	H W Beloe
1921/23	S H de la Courveuve
1923/24	C Smith
1924/25	A N Jones
1925/26	F J Press
1926/27	G H Clarke
1927/29	J S Harrison
1929/30	C W Beloe
1930/33	G H Clarke
1933/35	G Tryon
1935/37	W A D Alexander
1937/38	G S Sinnott
1938/39	Major N F Sampson-Way
1939/40	Captain G C Hardy, R N
1940/44	W A D Alexander
1944/45	C L Tivvy
1945/48	Colonel G L Stratton

1948/49	H T Williams
1949/52	R R S Harvey
1952/54	E C Abbott
1954/56	N S B Gwynn
1956/58	J F Robinson
1958/60	A L Taylor
1960/64	J E C Clarke
1964/65	W P Harris
1965/66	H E L Brown
1966/67	J D Ware
1967/69	G C Ehlers
1969/71	R M Davidson
1971/72	T J Hood
1972/74	H E L Brown
1974/76	W G Beloe
1976/78	N L Dallas
1978/80	J E Collins
1980/82	F R C Love
1982/84	D B Milliken-Smith
1984/85	A D Tasker
1985/87	R V S Castle
1987/89	R S Brooks
1989/91	M J Pople
1991/93	P T Beaham-Powell
1993/95	J B Moran
1995/97	J G Hordle
1997/99	C J Cave
1999/	T R Pearce